FIRST 50
DISNEY SONGS

YOU SHOULD PLAY ON UKULELE

The following songs in this publication are the property of:

Bourne Co.
Music Publishers
www.bournemusic.com

BABY MINE
GIVE A LITTLE WHISTLE
HEIGH-HO
I'VE GOT NO STRINGS
SOME DAY MY PRINCE WILL COME
WHEN YOU WISH UPON A STAR
WHISTLE WHILE YOU WORK
WHO'S AFRAID OF THE BIG BAD WOLF?

ISBN 978-1-5400-8646-4

HAL•LEONARD®

Visit Hal Leonard Online at
www.halleonard.com

Contact Us:
Hal Leonard
7777 West Bluemound Road
Milwaukee, WI 53213
Email: info@halleonard.com

In Europe, contact:
Hal Leonard Europe Limited
42 Wigmore Street
Marylebone, London, W1U 2RN
Email: info@halleonardeurope.com

In Australia, contact:
Hal Leonard Australia Pty. Ltd.
4 Lentara Court
Cheltenham, Victoria, 3192 Australia
Email: info@halleonard.com.au

CONTENTS

All Is Found

from FROZEN 2

Music and Lyrics by Kristen Anderson-Lopez and Robert Lopez

Chorus

Yes, she will sing to those who ___ hear; _____ and in her

song, _____ all mag - ic flows. _____ But can you brave what you most _

___ fear? ___ Can you face what the riv - er ___ knows? _____

Outro-Verse

___ Where the North - wind ___ meets the ___ sea, there's a

moth-er ___ full of ___ mem-o - ry. Come, my dar - ling, home-ward ___ bound. When all is

lost, then all ___ is ___ found. _____

Baby Mine

from DUMBO
Words by Ned Washington
Music by Frank Churchill

The Bare Necessities

from THE JUNGLE BOOK
Words and Music by Terry Gilkyson

Beauty and the Beast

from BEAUTY AND THE BEAST
Music by Alan Menken
Lyrics by Howard Ashman

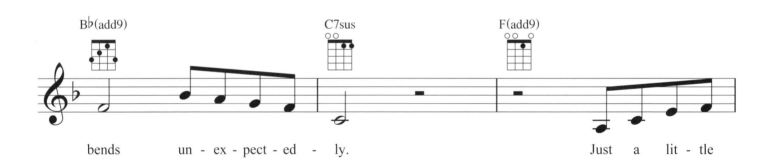

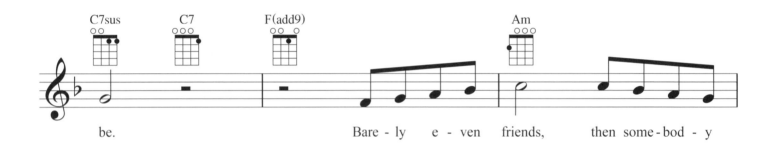

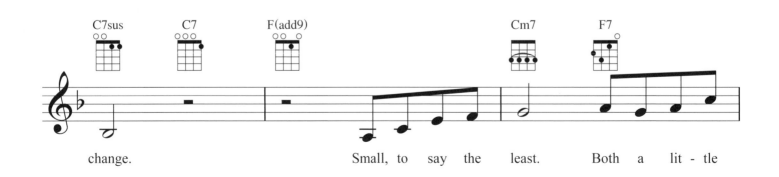

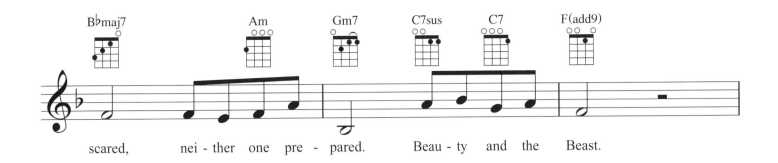

scared, nei - ther one pre - pared. Beau - ty and the Beast.

Bridge

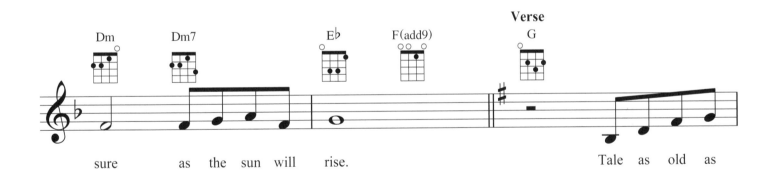

Ev - er just the same. Ev - er a sur -

prise. Ev - er as be - fore, ev - er just as

Verse

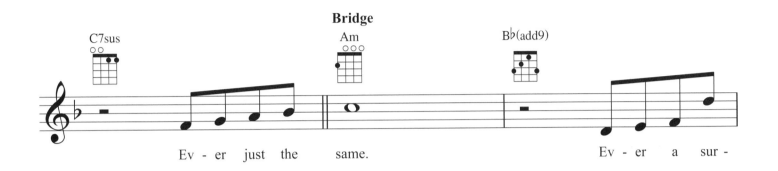

sure as the sun will rise. Tale as old as

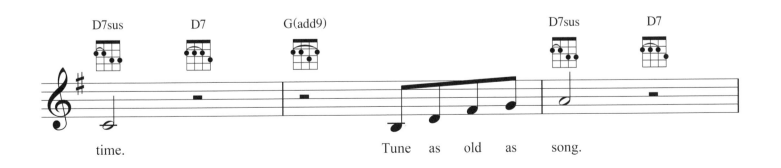

time. Tune as old as song.

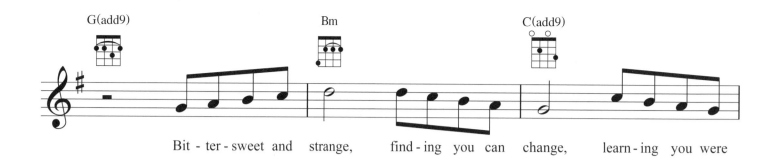

Bit - ter - sweet and strange, find - ing you can change, learn - ing you were

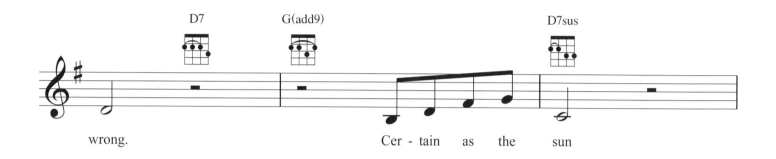

wrong. Cer - tain as the sun

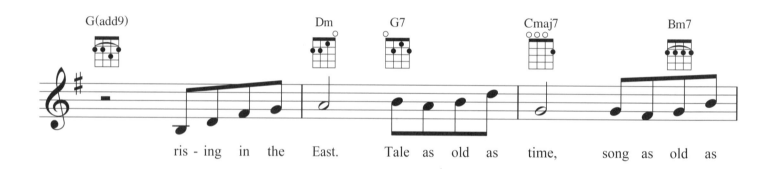

ris - ing in the East. Tale as old as time, song as old as

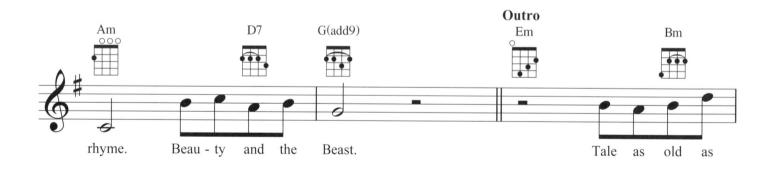

Outro

rhyme. Beau - ty and the Beast. Tale as old as

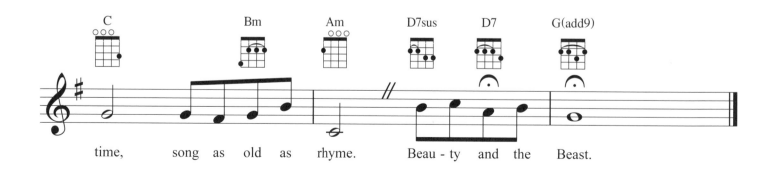

time, song as old as rhyme. Beau - ty and the Beast.

Bella Notte

from LADY AND THE TRAMP
Music and Lyrics by Peggy Lee and Sonny Burke

Chorus
Slowly

This ___ is the night, ___ it's a beau - ti - ful night, ___ and we

call it bel - la not - te. Look ___ at the skies; ___ they have

stars ___ in their eyes ___ on this love - ly bel - la not - te. So

take the love ___ of your loved one. You'll need it a - bout this time to

keep from fall - ing like a star ___ when you make that diz - zy climb. For

this ___ is the night ___ and the heav - ens are right ___ on this love - ly bel - la not - te.

Bibbidi-Bobbidi-Boo
(The Magic Song)

from CINDERELLA
Words by Jerry Livingston
Music by Mack David and Al Hoffman

First note

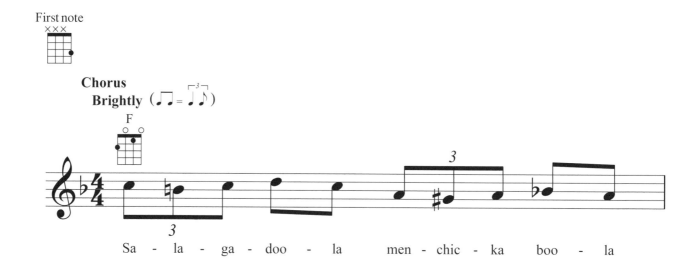

Chorus
Brightly

Sa - la - ga - doo - la   men - chic - ka   boo - la

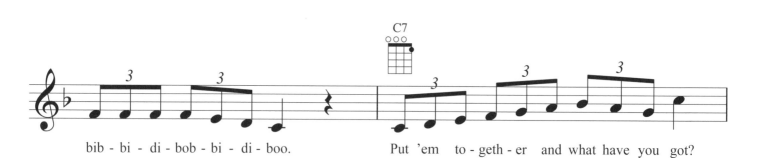

bib - bi - di - bob - bi - di - boo.   Put 'em to - geth - er and what have you got?

Chorus

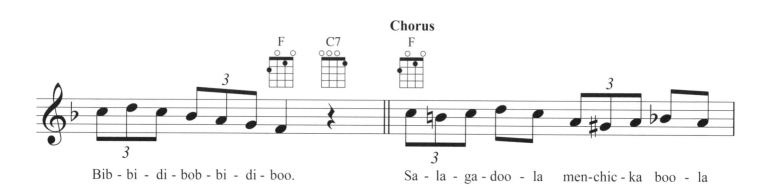

Bib - bi - di - bob - bi - di - boo.   Sa - la - ga - doo - la   men-chic - ka boo - la

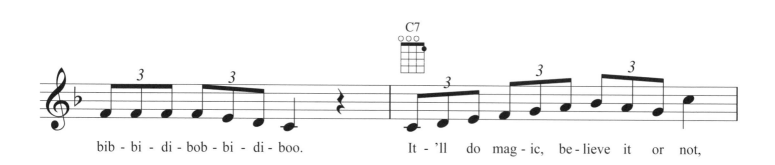

bib - bi - di - bob - bi - di - boo.   It - 'll do mag - ic, be - lieve it or not,

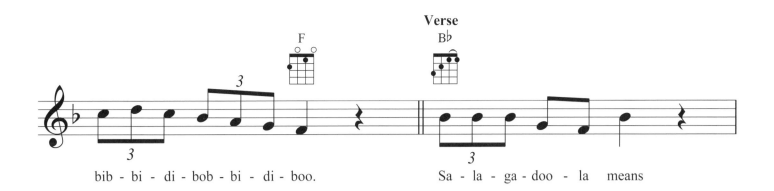

bib - bi - di - bob - bi - di - boo. Sa - la - ga - doo - la means

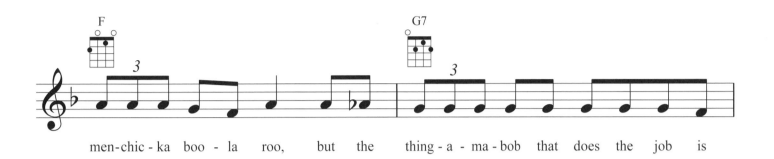

men - chic - ka boo - la roo, but the thing - a - ma - bob that does the job is

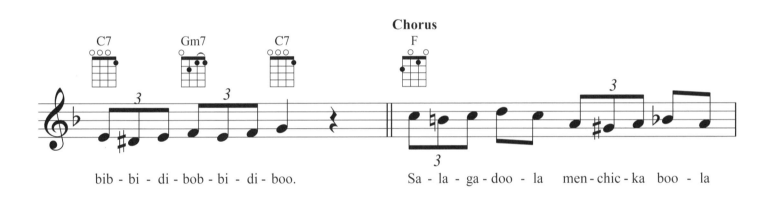

bib - bi - di - bob - bi - di - boo. Sa - la - ga - doo - la men - chic - ka boo - la

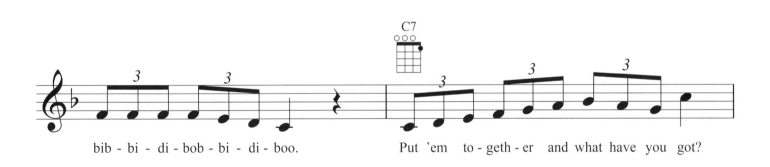

bib - bi - di - bob - bi - di - boo. Put 'em to - geth - er and what have you got?

Bib - bi - di - bob - bi - di, bib - bi - di - bob - bi - di, bib - bi - di - bob - bi - di - boo.

Can You Feel the Love Tonight

from THE LION KING
Music by Elton John
Lyrics by Tim Rice

1. There's a calm __ sur - ren - der   to the rush __ of   day,
2. There's a time __ for   ev - 'ry - one,   if they on - ly learn

when the heat __ of the roll - ing world __ can be turned __ a - way.
that the twist - ing ka - lei - do - scope __ moves us all ____ in turn.

An en - chant - ed   mo - ment,   and it sees __ me through.
There's a rhyme __ and   rea - son   to the wild __ out - doors

It's e - nough __ for this rest - less war - rior   just to be ____ with you. }
when the heart __ of this star - crossed voy - ag - er beats in time __ with yours. }   And

Chorus

can   you feel ____ the love ____ to - night? ____
can   you feel ____ the love ____ to - night, ____

Candle on the Water

from PETE'S DRAGON

Words and Music by Al Kasha and Joel Hirschhorn

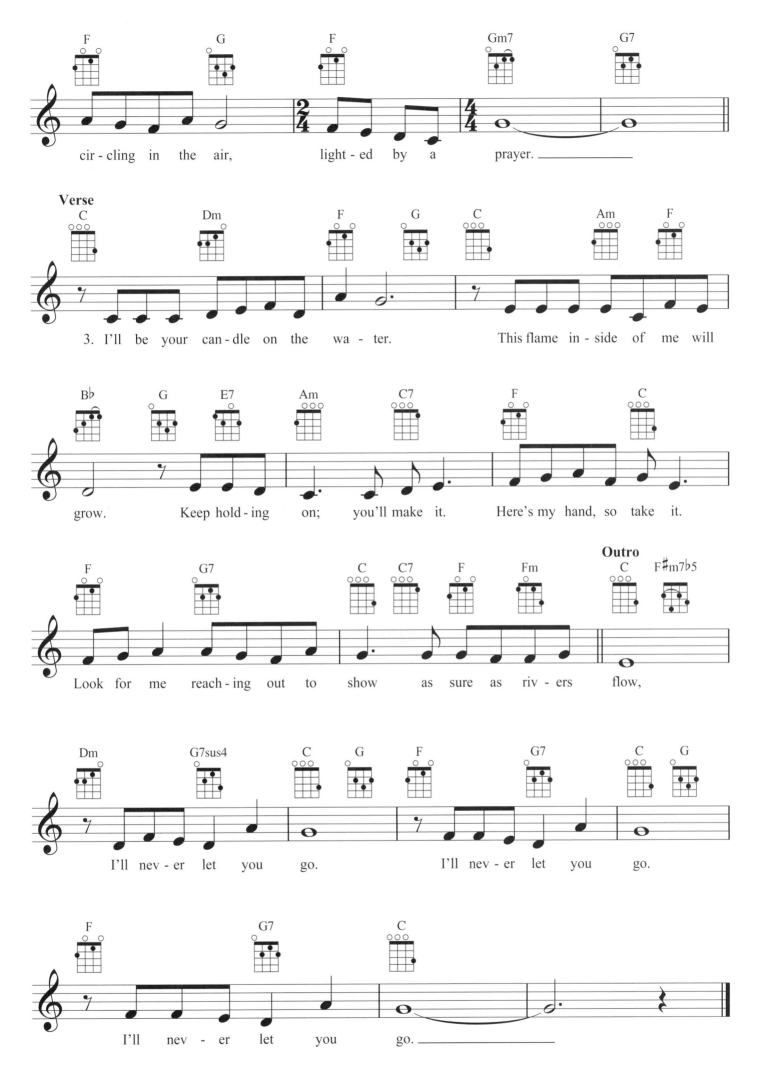

cir - cling in the air, light - ed by a prayer. _____

Verse

3. I'll be your can - dle on the wa - ter. This flame in - side of me will

grow. Keep hold - ing on; you'll make it. Here's my hand, so take it.

Outro

Look for me reach - ing out to show as sure as riv - ers flow,

I'll nev - er let you go. I'll nev - er let you go.

I'll nev - er let you go. _____

Chim Chim Cher-ee

from MARY POPPINS
Words and Music by Richard M. Sherman and Robert B. Sherman

Circle of Life

from THE LION KING
Music by Elton John
Lyrics by Tim Rice

find than can ev - er be found. ____ But the "Live and let live." ____ But

all are a - greed ___ as they join the stam - pede, ___ you should
sun roll - ing high ___ through the sap - phi - re sky ___ keeps great and

nev - er take more ___ than you give _____ in the cir - cle of life. __
small on the end - less ___ round ___ in the cir - cle of life. __

Chorus

It's the wheel of for - tune.

It's the leap of faith. ___ It's the band of ___ hope ___

'til we find ___ our __ place _____

Colors of the Wind

from POCAHONTAS
Music by Alan Menken
Lyrics by Stephen Schwartz

1. You think you own what-ev-er land you land on; the
(2.) think the on-ly peo-ple who are peo-ple are the
(3.) run the hid-den pine trails of the for-est, come
(4.) rain-storm and the riv-er are my broth-ers; the

earth is just a dead thing you can claim; but
peo - ple who look and think like you. But
taste the sun-sweet ber - ries of the earth, come
her - on and the ot - ter are my friends; and

I know ev - 'ry rock and tree and crea - ture has a
if you walk the foot-steps of a stran - ger, you'll learn
roll in all the rich - es all a - round you and, for
we are all con-nect - ed to each oth - er in a

1., 3.

life, has a spir - it, has a name. 2. You
once, nev - er won - der what they're worth. 4. The

Coda

Bridge

ends.   How   high   does   the   syc - a - more   grow?   If   you

cut   it   down,   then   you'll   nev - er   know.   And   you'll

Outro-Chorus

nev - er   hear the wolf cry   to   the   blue corn moon.   For wheth-er   we   are white or cop - per -

skinned,   we need to   sing with all   the   voic - es   of   the   moun - tain,   we   need to

paint with all   the   col - ors   of   the   wind.   You can   own the earth and, still,   all you'll

own is earth un - til   you can   paint with all   the   col - ors   of   the   wind.

Do You Want to Build a Snowman?

from FROZEN
Music and Lyrics by Kristen Anderson-Lopez and Robert Lopez

by.　(click tongue)　ANNA: (knocking)　(Spoken:) Elsa?

Verse

Slower, tenderly

3. Please, I know you're in there. Peo - ple are ask - ing where you've

been. They say, "Have cour - age," and I'm try - ing to; I'm right out

here for you, just let me in. We on - ly have each

oth - er; it's just you and me. ___ What are we gon - na do? ___

___ Do you want to build a snow - man?

Cruella De Vil

from 101 DALMATIANS
Words and Music by Mel Leven

First note

Verse

Slow Blues

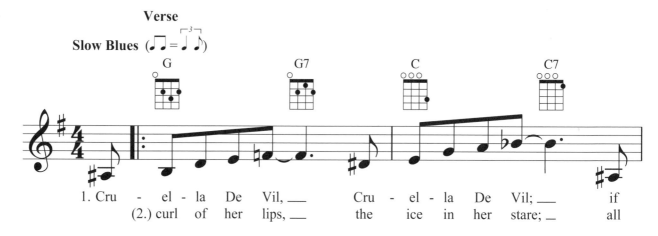

1. Cru - el - la De Vil, ___ Cru - el - la De Vil; ___ if
(2.) curl of her lips, ___ the ice in her stare; ___ all

she does - n't scare ___ you, no e - vil thing will. ___ To
in - no - cent chil - dren had bet - ter be - ware. ___ She's

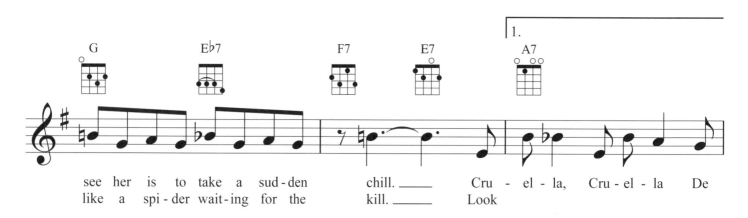

see her is to take a sud - den chill. ____ Cru - el - la, Cru - el - la De
like a spi - der wait - ing for the kill. ____ Look

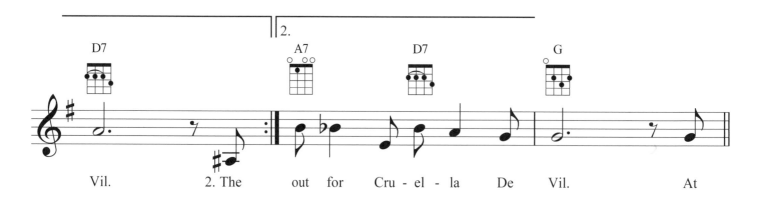

Vil. 2. The out for Cru - el - la De Vil. At

A Dream Is a Wish Your Heart Makes

from CINDERELLA
Music by Mack David and Al Hoffman
Lyrics by Jerry Livingston

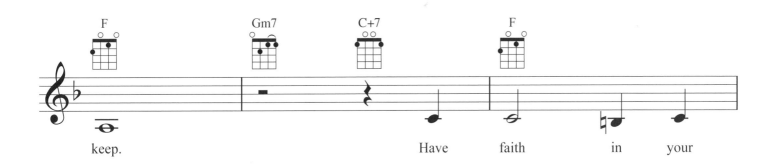

keep.   Have   faith   in   your

dreams   and   some   -   day _____   your

rain - bow   will   come   smil   -   ing   through. _____

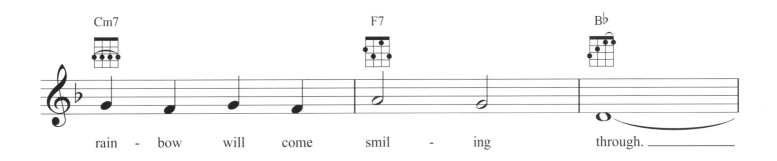

____   No   mat - ter   how   your   heart   is   griev - ing,   if

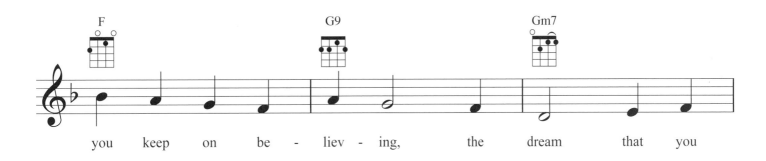

you   keep   on   be - liev - ing,   the   dream   that   you

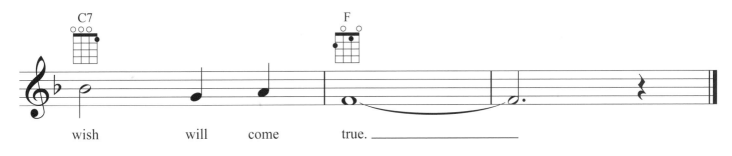

wish   will   come   true. _____

Evermore

from BEAUTY AND THE BEAST (2017)

Music by Alan Menken
Lyrics by Tim Rice

First note

Verse
Sturdy Ballad

1. I was the one ___ who had it all; ___

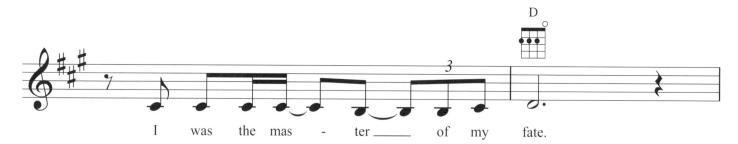

I was the mas - ter ___ of my fate.

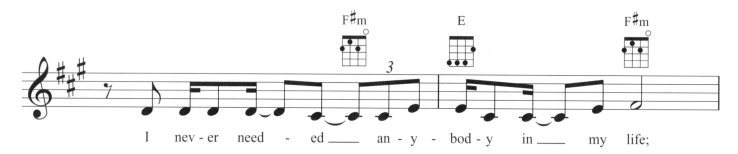

I nev - er need - ed ___ an - y - bod - y in ___ my life;

I learned the truth ___ too late.

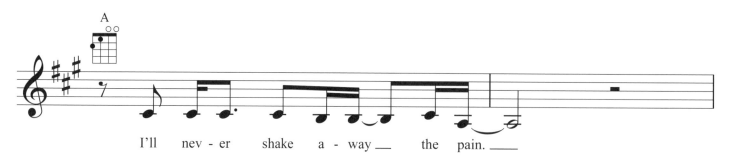

I'll nev - er shake a - way ___ the pain. ___

I close my eyes, __ but __ she's still there.

I let her steal __ in - to my mel - an - chol - y heart;

it's more than I can bear. _____ Now I

Chorus

know she'll nev - er leave me, e - ven as she runs a -

way. She will still tor - ment __ me, calm me, hurt __ me, move __

__ me, come __ what may. Wast - ing in __ my lone - ly

tow - er, _____ wait-ing by ___ an o - pen

door, I'll fool my - self she'll walk right

in, and be with me _____ for ev - er -

more.

Verse

2. I rage a - gainst ___ the trials of love.

I curse the fad - ing _____ of the light.

Heigh-Ho

from SNOW WHITE AND THE SEVEN DWARFS
Words by Larry Morey
Music by Frank Churchill

Give a Little Whistle

from PINOCCHIO
Words by Ned Washington
Music by Leigh Harline

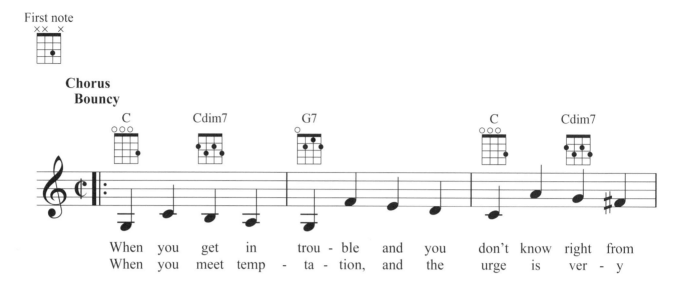

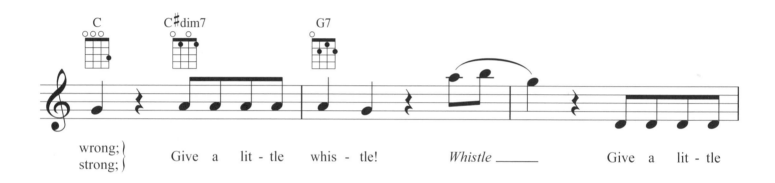

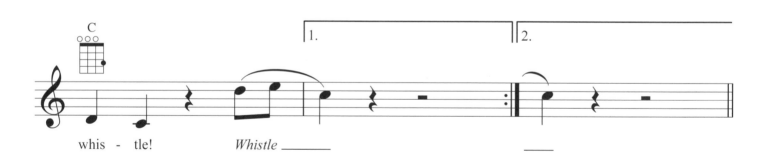

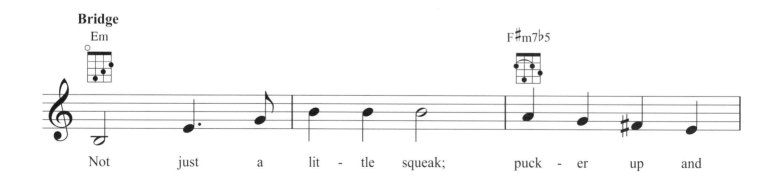

Chorus

blow.　And　if　your　whis - tle's　weak;

yell,　"Jim - i - ny　Crick - et."　Take　the　straight　and

nar - row　path　and　if　you　start　to　slide;　Give　a　lit - tle

whis - tle!　*Whistle _____*　Give　a　lit - tle

whis - tle!　*Whistle _____*　And　al - ways　let　your

con - science　be　your　guide.

Go the Distance

from HERCULES

Music by Alan Menken
Lyrics by David Zippel

God Help the Outcasts

from THE HUNCHBACK OF NOTRE DAME
Music by Alan Menken
Lyrics by Stephen Schwartz

Chorus

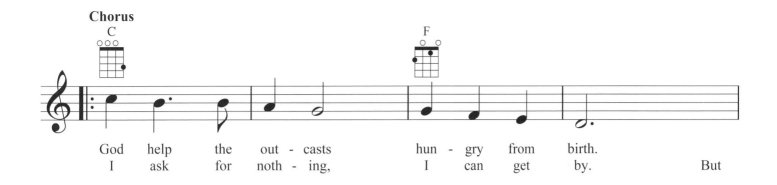

God help the out - casts hun - gry from birth.
I ask for noth - ing, I can get by. But

Show them the mer - cy they don't find on earth. The
I know so man - y less luck - y than I. The

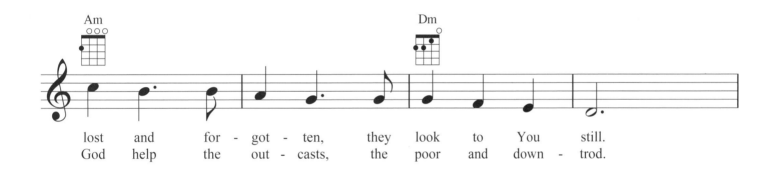

lost and for - got - ten, they look to You still.
God help the out - casts, the poor and down - trod.

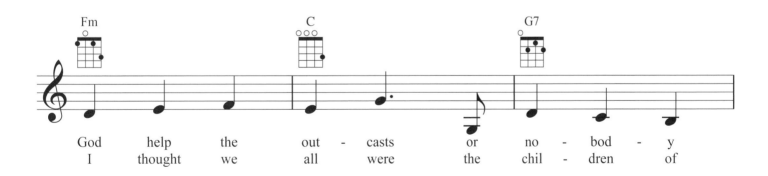

God help the out - casts or no - bod - y
I thought we all were the chil - dren of

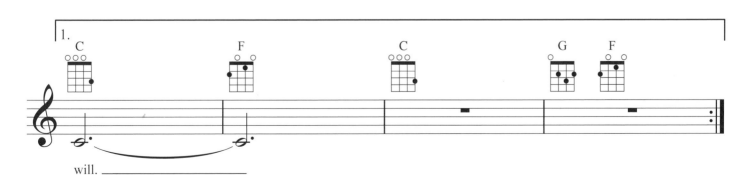

will. _____

Bridge

God.   I don't know if there's a

rea - son why some are blessed, some not.

Why the few You seem to fa - vor, _____ they

fear ___ us,   flee ___ us,   try ___ not to

Chorus

see us. _____   God help the out - casts, the

tat - tered, the torn,   seek - ing an

an - swer to why they were born. Winds of mis -

for - tune have blown them a - bout. You made the

out - casts; don't cast them out. The

Outro

poor and un - luck - y, the weak and the

odd; _____ I thought we all were the

chil - dren of God. _____

Hakuna Matata

from THE LION KING (2019)

Music by Elton John
Lyrics by Tim Rice

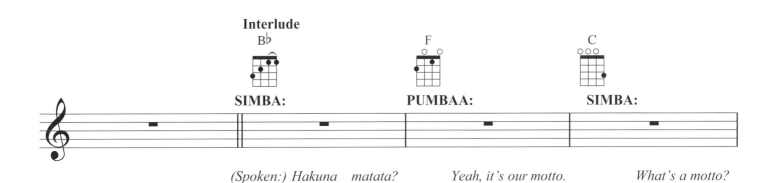

Interlude

SIMBA: PUMBAA: SIMBA:

(Spoken:) Hakuna matata? *Yeah, it's our motto.* *What's a motto?*

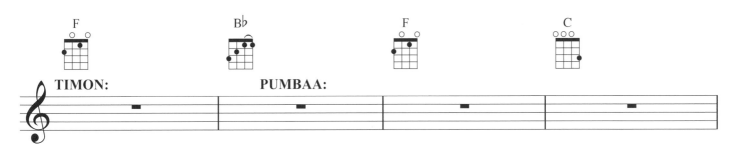

TIMON: PUMBAA:

Nothin'! What's - a - motto with you?! Nice! Boom! Those two words will solve all your problems.

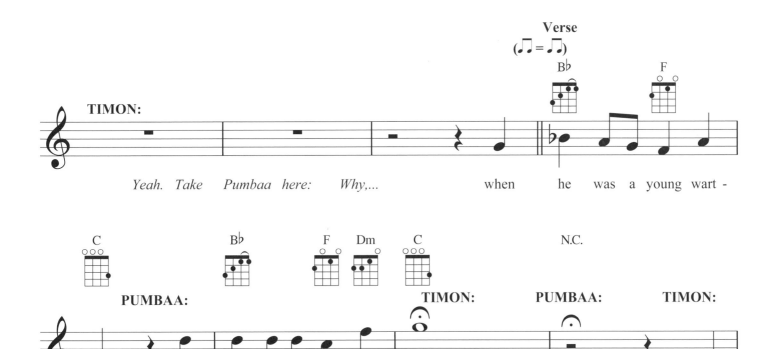

Verse

TIMON:

Yeah. Take Pumbaa here: Why,... when he was a young wart -

PUMBAA: TIMON: PUMBAA: TIMON:

hog... When I was a young wart - hog! *How ya feelin'? It's an emotional story.* He

(Spoken:)

found his a - ro - ma lacked a cer - tain ap - peal. ___ He could clear the sa - van - nah af - ter

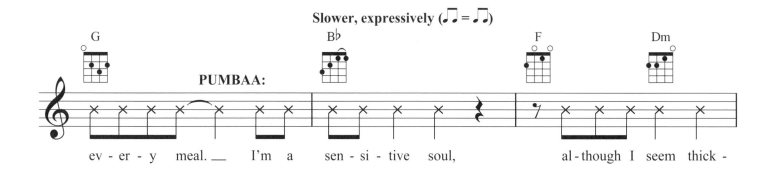

ev - er - y meal. __ I'm a sen - si - tive soul, al - though I seem thick -

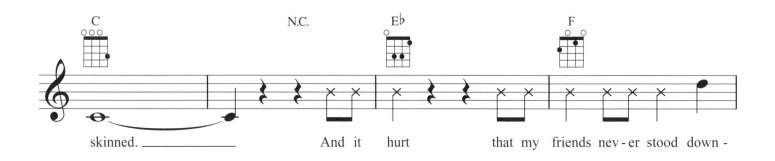

skinned. _____ And it hurt that my friends nev - er stood down -

wind! _____ And oh! __ The shame! Yes, he was a -

TIMON:
(Spoken:) I was always here for you, and I resent that!

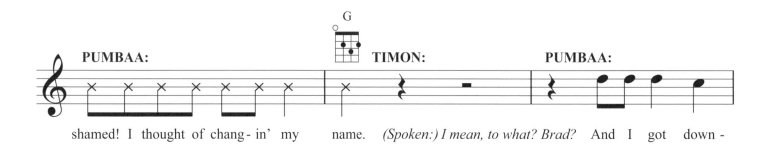

shamed! I thought of chang - in' my name. *(Spoken:) I mean, to what? Brad?* And I got down -

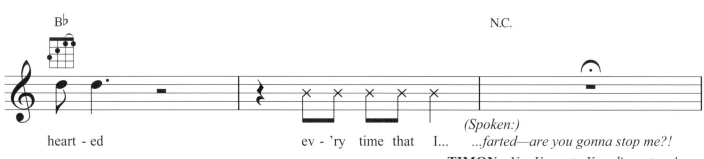

heart - ed ev - 'ry time that I... *(Spoken:)* ...*farted—are you gonna stop me?!*

TIMON: *No, I'm not. You disgust me!*

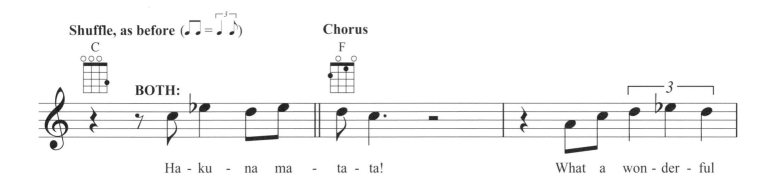

Shuffle, as before (♫ = ♩♪) Chorus

BOTH:

Ha - ku - na ma - ta - ta! What a won - der - ful

phrase. Ha - ku - na ma - ta - ta

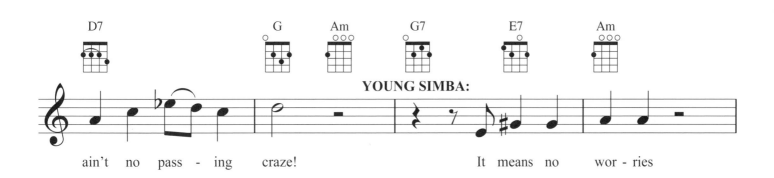

YOUNG SIMBA:

ain't no pass - ing craze! It means no wor - ries

PUMBAA: **YOUNG SIMBA & TIMON:**

for the rest ___ of your days. ___ *(Spoken:) Yeah, sing it, kid!* It's our

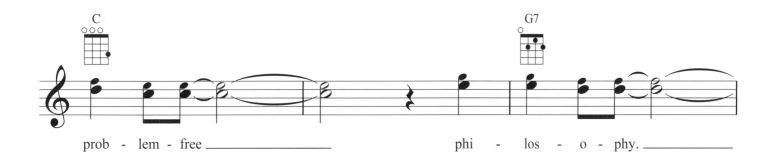

prob - lem - free _____ phi - los - o - phy. _____

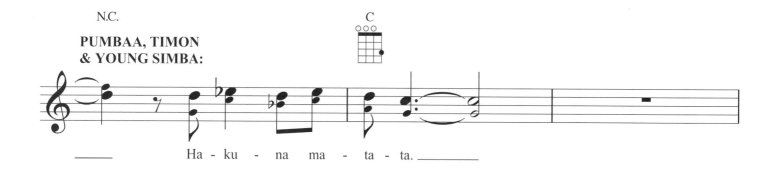

PUMBAA, TIMON
& YOUNG SIMBA:

Ha - ku - na ma - ta - ta. _____

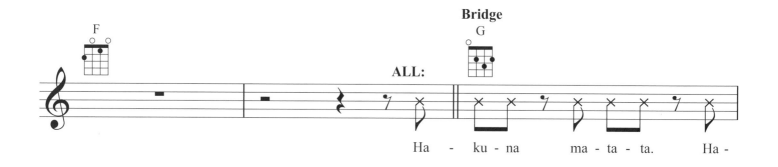

Bridge

ALL:

Ha - ku - na ma - ta - ta. Ha -

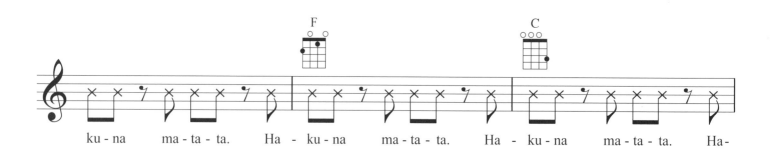

ku - na ma - ta - ta. Ha - ku - na ma - ta - ta. Ha - ku - na ma - ta - ta. Ha -

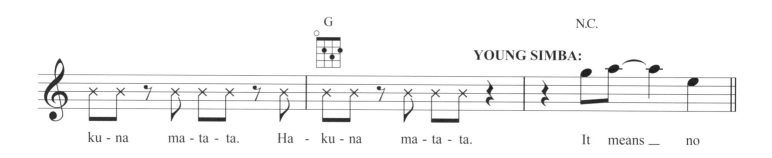

YOUNG SIMBA:

ku - na ma - ta - ta. Ha - ku - na ma - ta - ta. It means __ no

Outro-Chorus

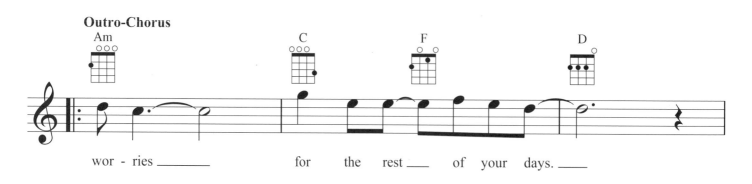

wor - ries _____ for the rest __ of your days. __

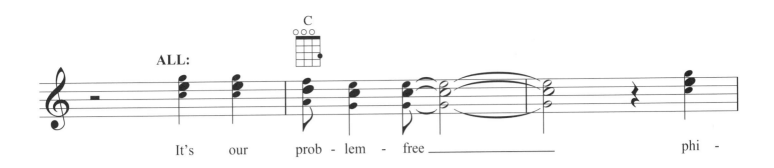

ALL: It's our prob - lem - free _____ phi -

1.

los - o - phy. __ YOUNG SIMBA: Ha - ku - na ma - ta - ta. _____

Ha - ku - na ma - ta - ta, _____ yeah. _____ Ha - ku - na ma -

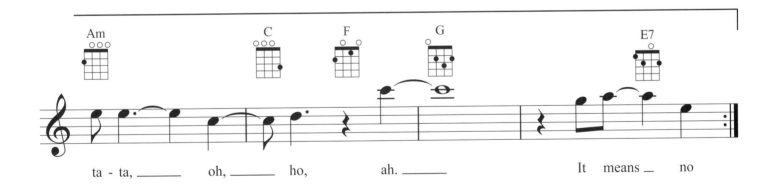

ta - ta, _____ oh, _____ ho, _____ ah. _____ It means _ no

2.
N.C.

YOUNG SIMBA: Ha - ku - na ma - ta - ta. _____

He's a Tramp

from LADY AND THE TRAMP

Words and Music by Peggy Lee and Sonny Burke

First note

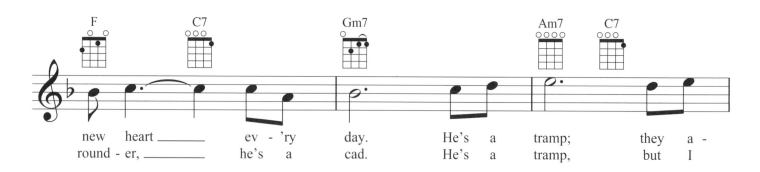

1. He's a tramp, but they love him; _____ breaks a
   tramp, he's a scoun - drel; _____ he's a

new heart _____ ev - 'ry day. He's a tramp; they a -
round - er, _____ he's a cad. He's a tramp, but I

1.

dore him, _____ and I on - ly hope he'll stay that way. 2. He's a
love him. _____ Yes, _____

2.

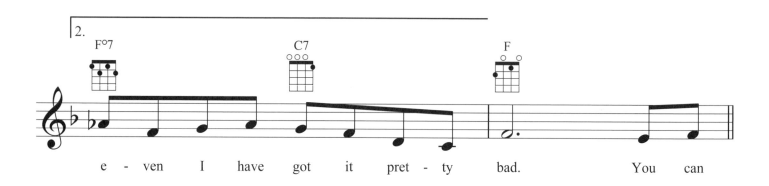

e - ven I have got it pret - ty bad. You can

How Does a Moment Last Forever

from BEAUTY AND THE BEAST (2017)
Music by Alan Menken
Lyrics by Tim Rice

1. How does a mo-ment last for-ev-er? _____ How can a sto-ry nev-er

die? It is love we must hold on to; nev-er

eas-y, but we try. Some-times our hap-pi-ness is

cap-tured; _____ some-how, a time and place stand still.

Love lives on _____ in-side our hearts _____ and al-ways will.

Min - utes turn to ho - urs; days to years, __ then __

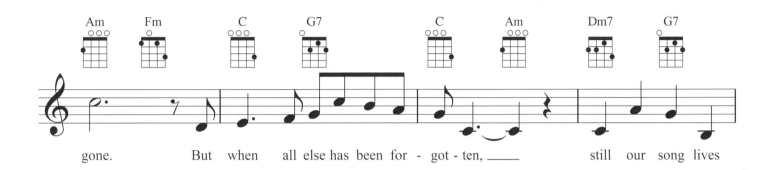

gone. But when all else has been for - got - ten, _____ still our song lives

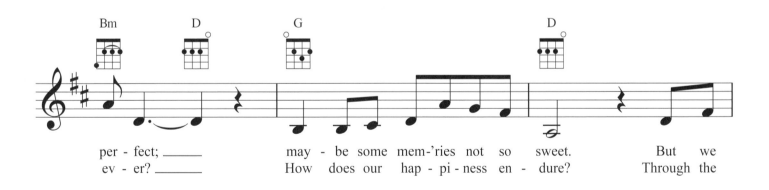

𝄋 **Verse**

on.

2. May - be some mo - ments weren't so
3. How does a mo - ment last for -

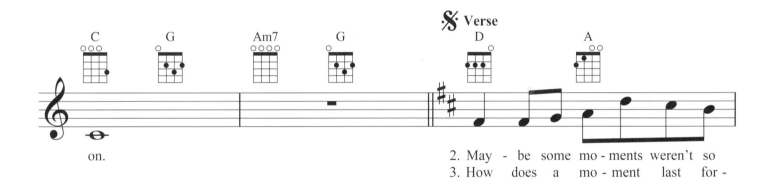

per - fect; _____ may - be some mem - 'ries not so sweet. But we
ev - er? _____ How does our hap - pi - ness en - dure? Through the

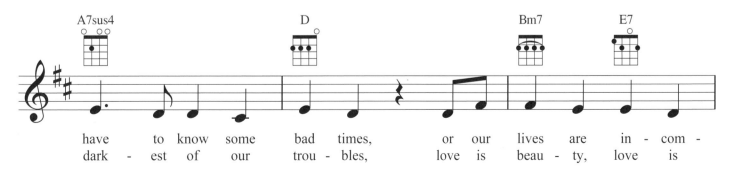

have to know some bad times, or our lives are in - com -
dark - est of our trou - bles, love is beau - ty, love is

plete.
pure.

Then, when the shad - ows o - ver - take us, _____
Love pays no mind to des - o - la - tion; _____ it

just when we feel all hope is gone, we'll hear our song and know _
flows like a riv - er through the soul, pro - tects, pro - ceeds and per -

To Coda ⊕

Interlude

_____ once more, _ our love lives _ on. *(Instrumental)*
- se - veres, _ and

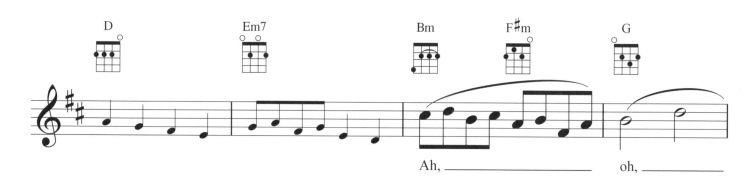

Ah, _____ oh, _____

D.S. al Coda

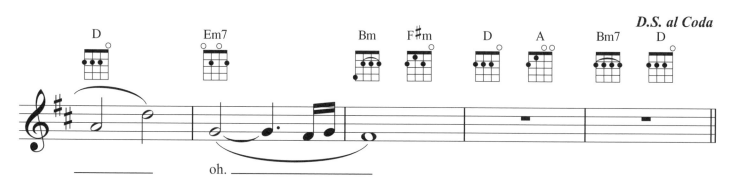

_____ oh. _____

Coda

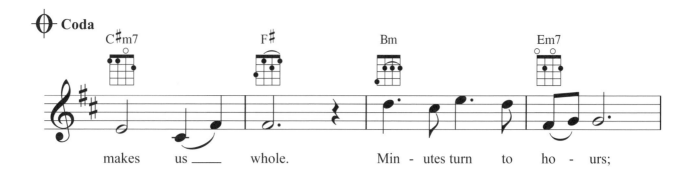

makes us ___ whole. Min - utes turn to ho - urs;

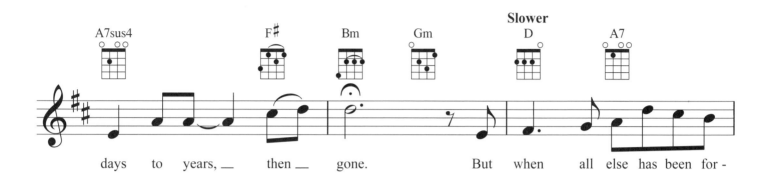

days to years, ___ then ___ gone. But when all else has been for-

got - ten, ___ still our song lives ___ on. ___

Outro

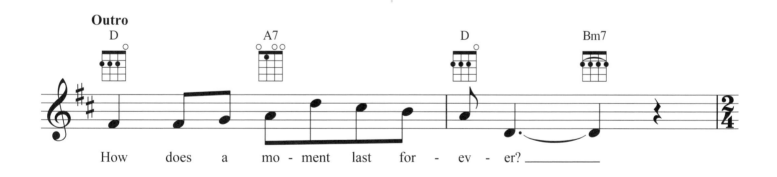

How does a mo - ment last for - ev - er? ___

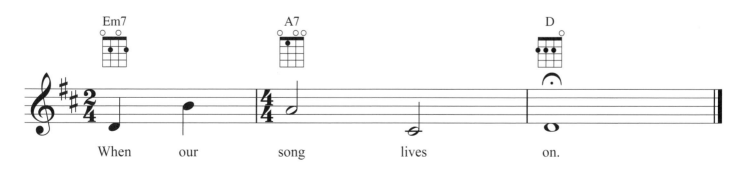

When our song lives on.

How Far I'll Go

from MOANA
Music and Lyrics by Lin-Manuel Miranda

First note

Verse
Moderately

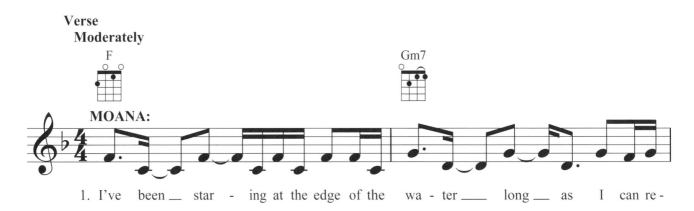

MOANA:

1. I've been __ star - ing at the edge of the wa - ter __ long __ as I can re-

mem - ber, __ nev - er real - ly know - ing why.

I wish __ I could be the per - fect daugh - ter, __ but I come back to the

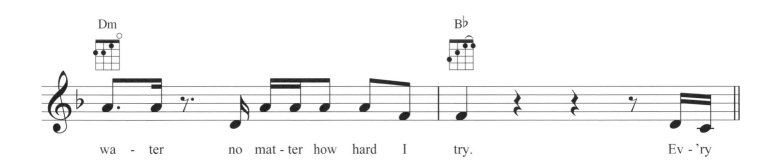

wa - ter no mat - ter how hard I try. Ev - 'ry

Verse

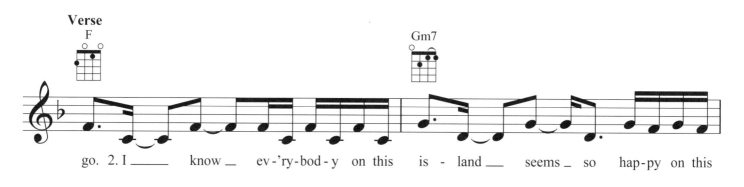

go. 2. I _____ know _____ ev-'ry-bod-y on this is - land _____ seems _ so hap-py on this

is - land. __ Ev - 'ry - thing is by de - sign. __

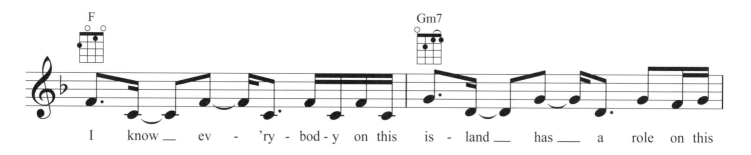

I know __ ev - 'ry - bod - y on this is - land __ has __ a role on this

is - land, __ so may-be I can roll with mine. __ I can

Pre-Chorus

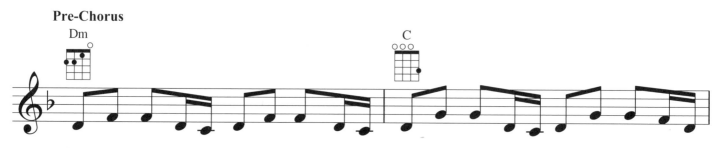

lead with pride, I can make us strong. I'll be sat - is - fied if I play a - long, but the

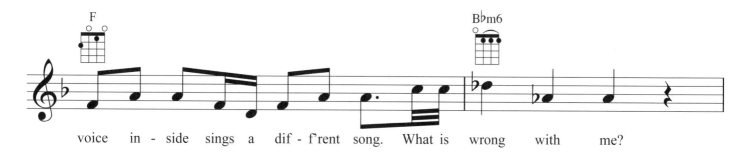

voice in - side sings a dif - f'rent song. What is wrong with me?

Chorus

See the light as it shines on the sea: it's blind -
line where the sky meets the sea, it calls _

- ing, but no one knows _____ how deep it
_ me, and no one knows _____ how far it

goes. _____ And it seems like it's call-ing out to me, so come find _
goes. _____ If the wind in my sail _ on the sea stays be-hind _

1.
_ me, and let me know. _____ What's be -
_ me, one day I'll

2.
yond that line? Will I cross that line? The know _____ how far I'll

go! _____

I Just Can't Wait to Be King

from THE LION KING

Music by Elton John
Lyrics by Tim Rice

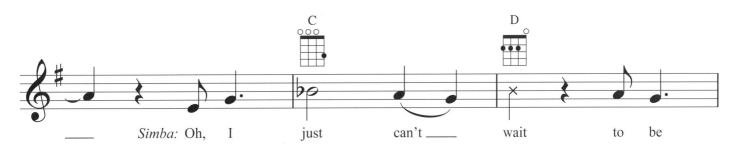

Simba: Oh, I just can't ____ wait to be

king!   _Zazu (Spoken:)_   _You've rather a long way to go, young master! If you think..._   _Simba:_ No one say - ing

Chorus

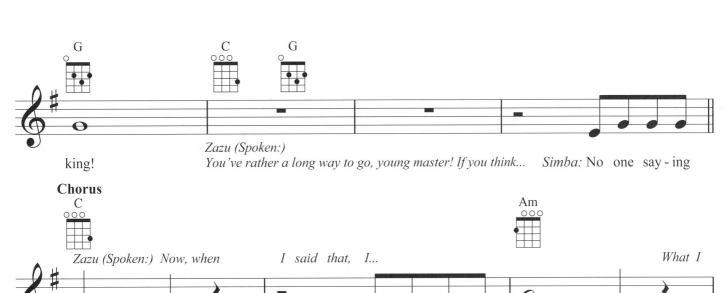

Zazu (Spoken:) Now, when   I said that, I...   _What I_

"do   this,"   no   one   say - ing   "be   there,"

meant was that the...   _But what you don't realize..._

no   one   say - ing   "stop   that,"   no   one   say - ing

Now   see   here!

"see   here." ____   Free   to   run   a - round   all ____

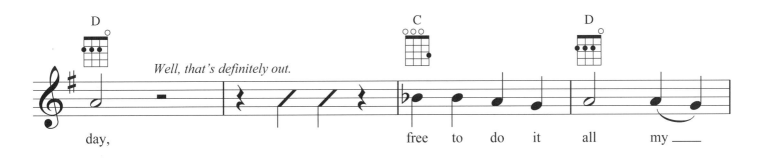

Well, that's definitely out.

day,   free   to   do   it   all   my ____

way!   *Zazu:* 2. I

Verse

think   it's   time   that   you   and   I   ar - ranged   a   heart - to -

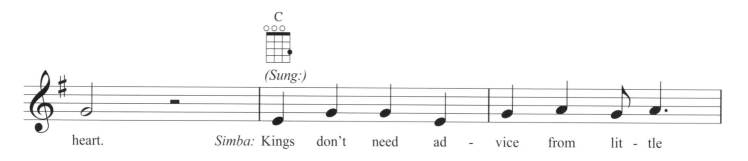

(Sung:)

heart.   *Simba:* Kings   don't   need   ad - vice   from   lit - tle

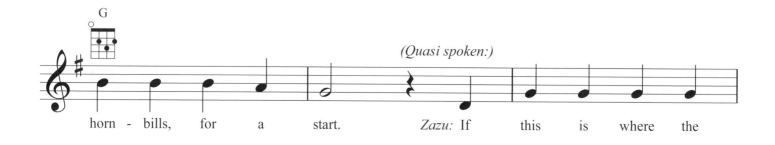

(Quasi spoken:)

horn - bills,   for   a   start.   *Zazu:* If   this   is   where   the

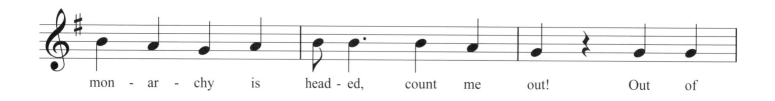

mon - ar - chy   is   head - ed,   count   me   out!   Out   of

ser - vice,   out   of   Af - ri - ca. ___   I   would - n't   hang   a -

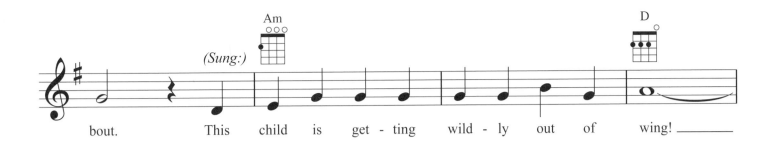

bout. This child is get - ting wild - ly out of wing! _____

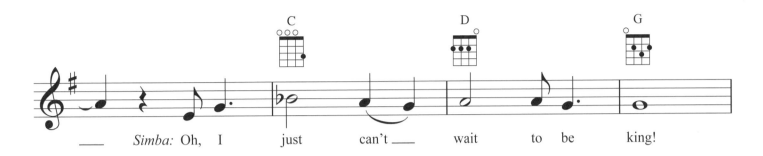

_____ *Simba:* Oh, I just can't ___ wait to be king!

Chorus

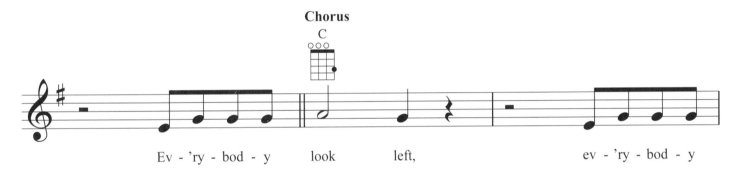

Ev - 'ry - bod - y look left, ev - 'ry - bod - y

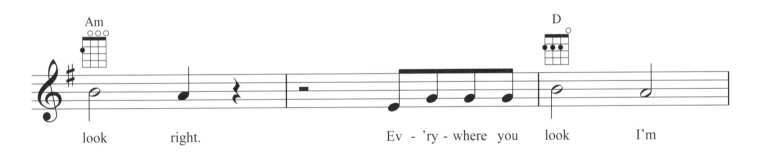

look right. Ev - 'ry - where you look I'm

Zazu (Spoken:)
Not yet!

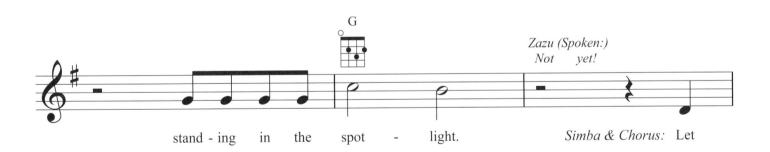

stand - ing in the spot - light. *Simba & Chorus:* Let

ev - 'ry crea - ture go for broke ___ and sing. _____ Let's

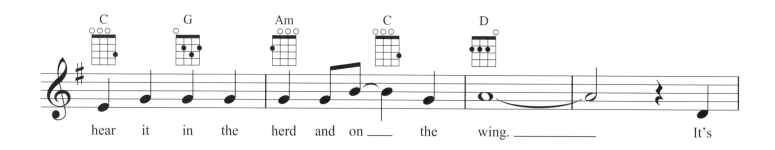

hear it in the herd and on ___ the wing. _____ It's

gon - na be King Sim - ba's fin - est fling. *Simba:* Oh, I

just can't ___ wait to be king. Oh, I

just can't ___ wait to be king. Oh, I

Outro

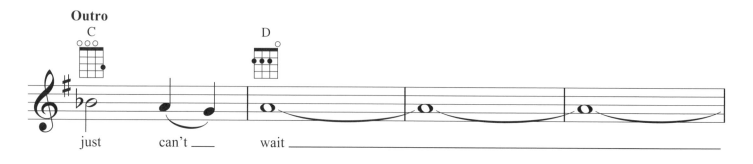

just can't ___ wait _____

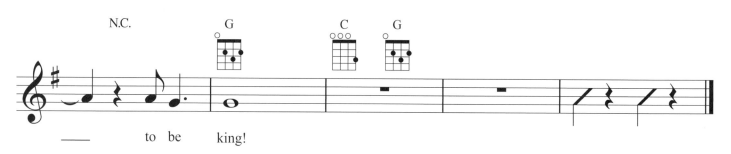

___ to be king!

I've Got No Strings

from PINOCCHIO
Words by Ned Washington
Music by Leigh Harline

I See the Light

from TANGLED
Music by Alan Menken
Lyrics by Glenn Slater

Chorus

light, *Female:* and it's like the sky is new. *Both:* And it's

warm and real ___ and bright, ___ and the world has some - how

Outro-Verse
Expressively

shift - ed. All at once,

ev - 'ry - thing is dif - f'rent, now that I see you.

Slowly, freely

Now that I see

you.

If I Never Knew You
(End Title)

from POCAHONTAS
Music by Alan Menken
Lyrics by Stephen Schwartz

Pre-Chorus

F | Dm | G7sus4 | G7

me. _____ In this world so full of fear, ___

Dm | G7sus4 | G7 | Em7 | E7

full of rage and lies, I can see ___ the

Am | F | G | G7sus4

truth so clear ___ in your eyes, ___ so dry your eyes. ___

Chorus

C | Am | C

And I'm so grate - ful to you. I'd have lived ___ my

C | F | Dm | C | F | G7sus4 | F

whole life through, lost for - ev - er if I nev - er knew you. ___

Verse

G | F | G | C | Am

(Instrumental)   *Female:* 3. If I nev - er knew you,

Outro-Chorus

bright. _____ *Female:* I thought our love would be so beau-ti-ful,

we'd turn the dark-ness in-to light. _____ *Both:* And still my heart is say-ing we were

right. _____ *Male:* We were right. And if I nev-er

knew you, I'd have lived my whole life through

Female: emp-ty as ___ the sky, *Both:* nev-er know - ing why, _____

Freely

lost for-ev - er if I nev-er knew you.

Kiss the Girl

from THE LITTLE MERMAID
Music by Alan Menken
Lyrics by Howard Ashman

Chorus

Sha la la la la la, my oh my. __ Look like the boy too shy. __ Ain't gon-na

kiss the girl.   Sha la la la la la, ain't that sad. __ Ain't it a

shame, too bad. __ He gon-na miss the girl. __   *(Instrumental)*

Verse

3. Now's your mo - ment,   float-ing in a blue la - goon. __

__ Boy, you bet-ter do it soon. __ No time will be

bet - ter. __   She don't say a word __ and she won't __

Into the Unknown

from FROZEN 2

Music and Lyrics by Kristen Anderson-Lopez and Robert Lopez

* Recorded a half step higher.

nore your whis - pers, ___ which I wish would go a - way... _____ Oh. ___

___ (Ah. _____ Oh. _____ Ah.) _____

Verse
With determination

2. You're _ not a voice, you're just a

ring - ing in my ear, ___ and ___ if I heard you, ___ which I don't, I'm

spo - ken for, ___ I ___ fear. Ev - 'ry - one I've ev - er loved is

here with - in these walls. _ I'm sor - ry, se - cret si - ren, but I'm

block-ing out your calls. ___ I've had my ad - ven - ture. I

don't need some - thing new! ___ I'm a - fraid of what I'm risk - ing if I

Chorus

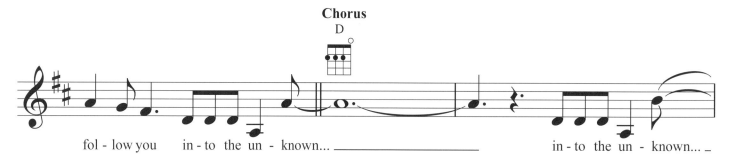

fol - low you in - to the un - known... _____ in - to the un - known... _

_____ in - to the un - known! _____

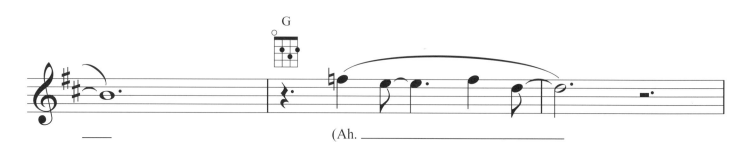

(Ah. _____

Ah.) _____ 3. What ___ do you

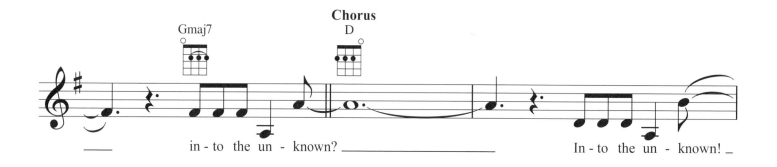

Chorus

in - to the un - known? _____ In - to the un - known! _

_____ In - to the un - known! _____

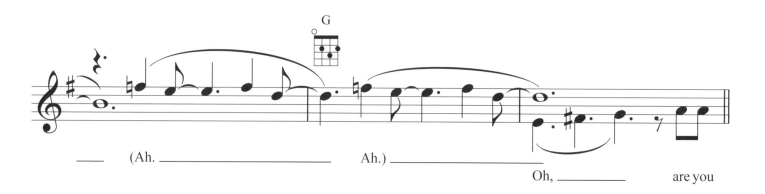

___ (Ah. _____ Ah.) _____ Oh, _____ are you

Bridge

out there? Do you know me? Can you feel me? Can you show me? _____

Interlude

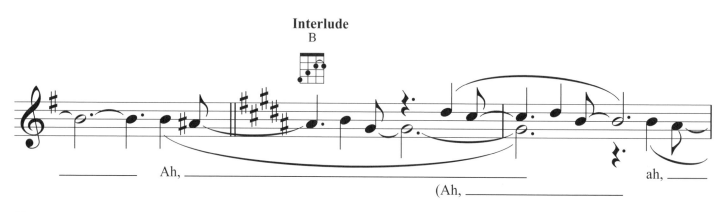

_____ Ah, _____ ah, _____

(Ah, _____

ah, _____
ah, _____

ah, _____   ah, _____
ah, _____   ah, _____

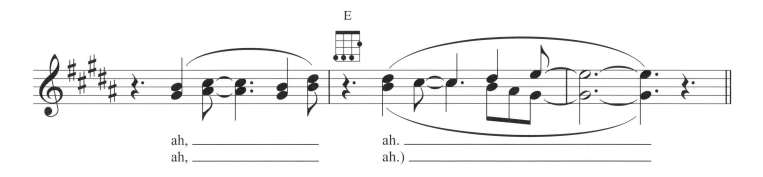

ah, _____   ah. _____
ah, _____   ah.) _____

Outro

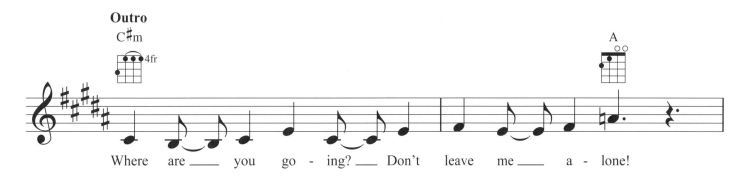

Where are ___ you go - ing? ___ Don't leave me ___ a - lone!

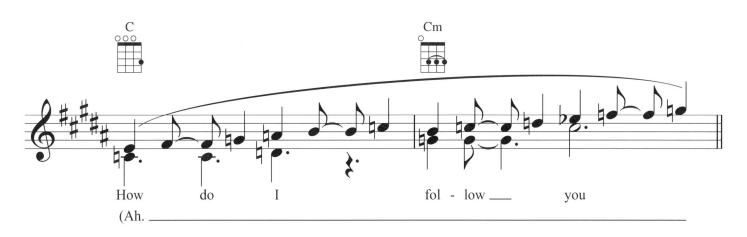

How   do   I   fol - low ___ you
(Ah. _____

Dramatically

in - to the ___ un - known?
Ah.) _____

89

It's a Small World

from Disney Parks' "it's a small world" attraction
Words and Music by Richard M. Sherman and Robert B. Sherman

Lava

from LAVA
Music and Lyrics by James Ford Murphy

And from his la-va came _ this song of hope
Now she was so read - y ____ to meet ____ him a -

that he sang _ out loud ev-'ry day ___ for years _ and
bove the sea _ as he sang his song of hope ___ for the ___ last

Chorus

(2nd time: slower)

years.
time.

"I have a dream ___ I

hope will ___ come true, that you're here ___ with me and

I'm here ___ with you. I wish that ___ the earth, sea ___ and the

sky up ___ a - bove - a will send me some - one to

To Coda

Chorus

Both: "I have a dream ___ I hope will ___ come

true, *Male:* (Ooh.) ___ and I'll grow old with you. ___
Female: that you'll grow old with me, ___ (Ah.) ___

___ *Both:* We thank ___ the earth, sea, ___ and the sky we ___ thank, ___

too. I la - va you.

I la - va you. ___

rit. I la - va you." ___

Let It Go

from FROZEN

Music and Lyrics by Kristen Anderson-Lopez and Robert Lopez

First note

Verse
Half-time feel, mysterious

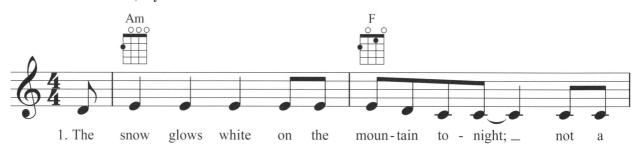

1. The snow glows white on the moun-tain to-night; — not a

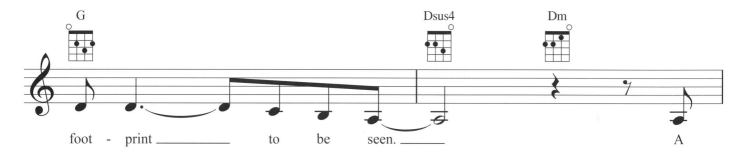

foot - print ____ to be seen. ____

king - dom of i - so - la - tion, and it

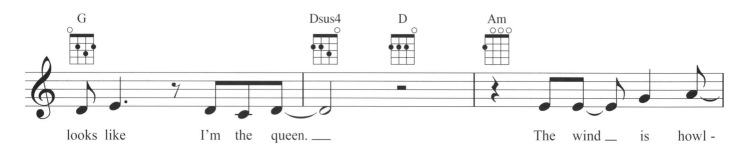

looks like I'm the queen. ____ The wind ___ is howl-

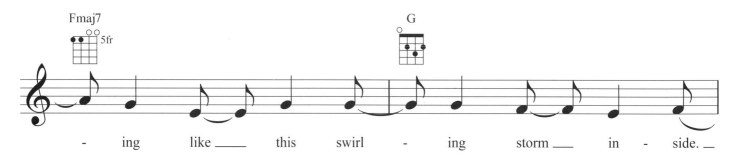

- ing like ____ this swirl - ing storm ___ in - side. ___

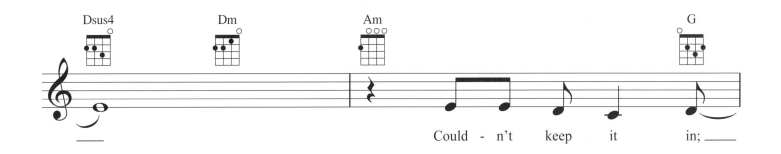

Could - n't keep it in; ____

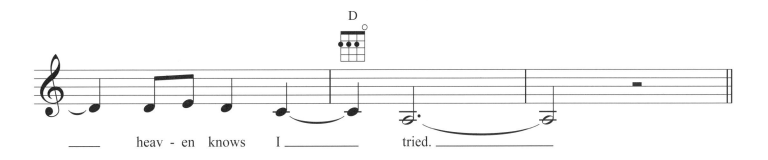

____ heav - en knows I ____ tried. ____

Pre-Chorus

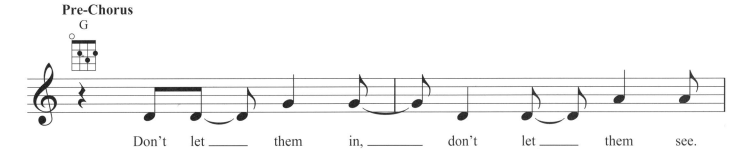

Don't let ____ them in, ____ don't let ____ them see.

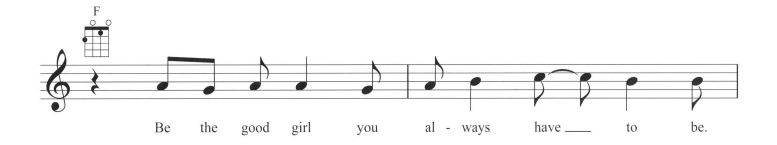

Be the good girl you al - ways have ____ to be.

Con - ceal, __ don't feel, don't let ____ them know... ____

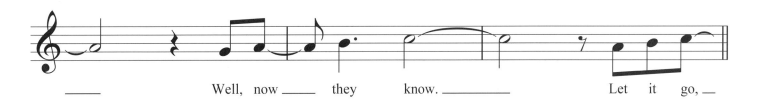

____ Well, now ____ they know. ____ Let it go, __

The cold nev - er both - ered me an -

Gaining confidence

y - way.

Verse

2. It's fun - ny how some dis - tance makes

ev - 'ry - thing ___ seem small; ___ and the

fears that once ___ con - trolled ___ me can't

Pre-Chorus

get to me ___ at all. ___ It's time ___ to see ___

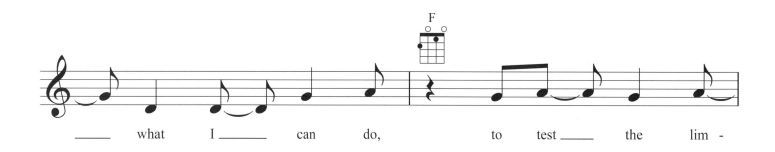

what I _____ can do, to test _____ the lim -

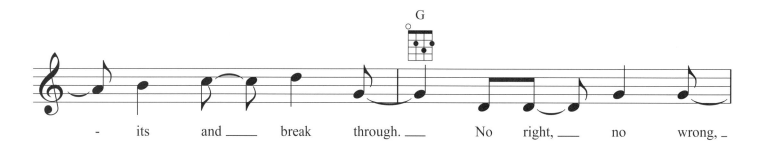

- its and _____ break through. _____ No right, _____ no wrong, _____

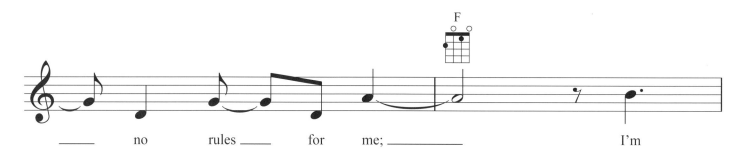

_____ no rules _____ for me; _____ I'm

D.S. al Coda

free! _____ Let it go, _____

Bridge

My pow - er flur - ries through _ the air _____

_____ in - to _____ the ground. _____ My soul _ is spi -

-ral - ing _____ in fro - zen frac - tals all _____

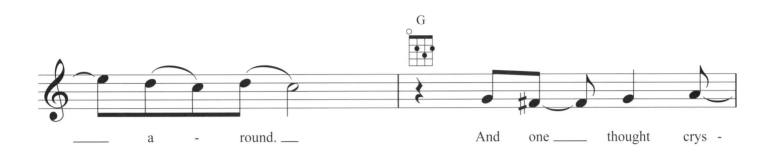

_____ a - round. _____ And one _____ thought crys -

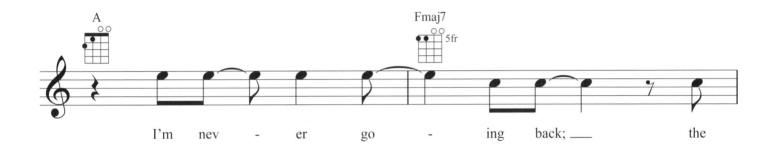

- tal - liz - es like _____ an i - cy blast: _____

I'm nev - er go - ing back; _____ the

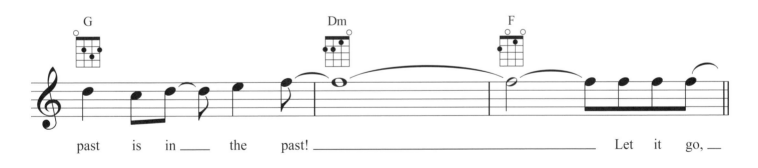

past is in _____ the past! _____ Let it go, _____

Chorus

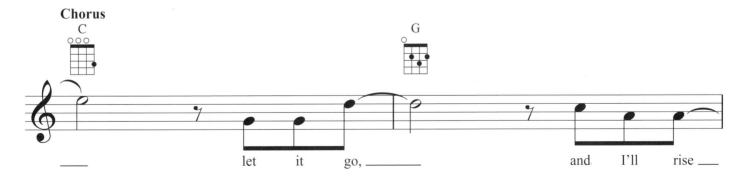

_____ let it go, _____ and I'll rise _____

Mickey Mouse March

from THE MICKEY MOUSE CLUB
Words and Music by Jimmie Dodd

The Place Where Lost Things Go

from MARY POPPINS RETURNS
Music by Marc Shaiman
Lyrics by Scott Wittman and Marc Shaiman

*Originally in A major.

Bridge

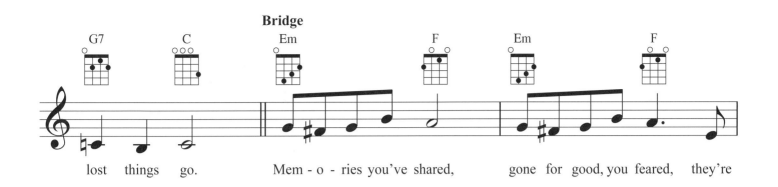

lost things go.   Mem - o - ries you've shared,   gone for good, you feared,   they're

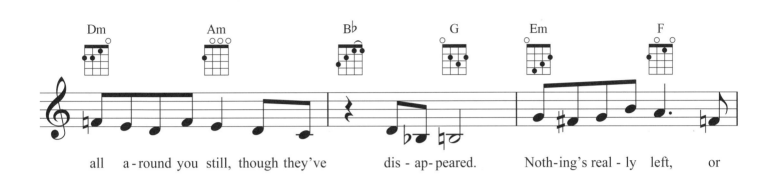

all   a - round you still, though they've   dis - ap - peared.   Noth - ing's real - ly left,   or

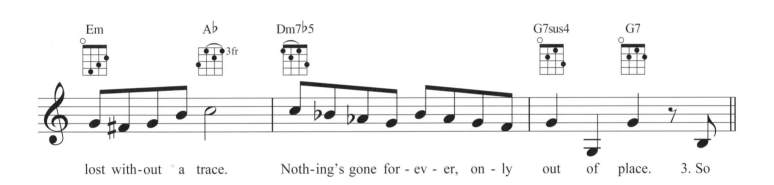

lost with - out a trace.   Noth - ing's gone for - ev - er, on - ly   out   of   place.   3. So

Verse

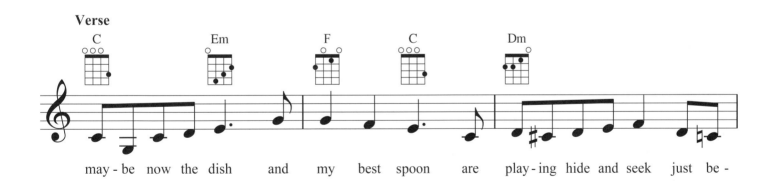

may - be now the dish   and   my   best spoon   are   play - ing hide and seek   just be -

hind   the   moon,   wait - ing there un - til   it's   time   to   show.

Spring is like that now,   far be-neath the snow,   hid-ing in the place where the

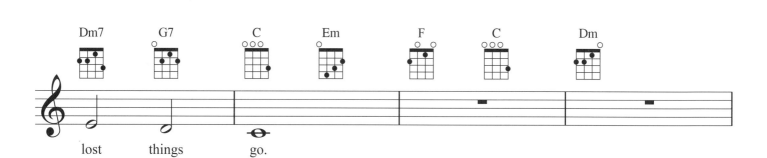

lost   things   go.

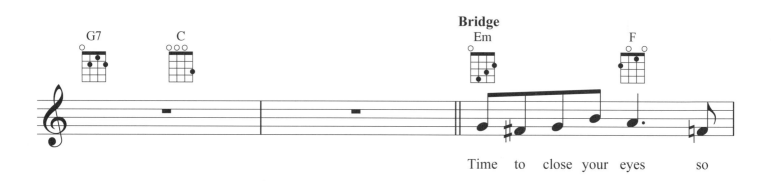

Bridge

Time to close your eyes   so

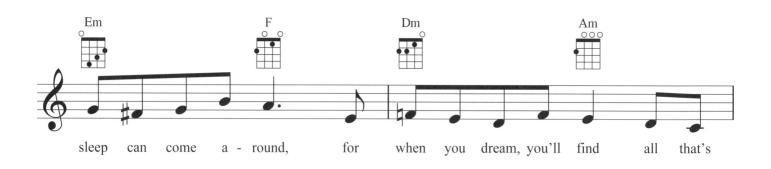

sleep can come a-round,   for when you dream, you'll find   all that's

lost is found.   May-be on the moon,   or   may-be some-where new,

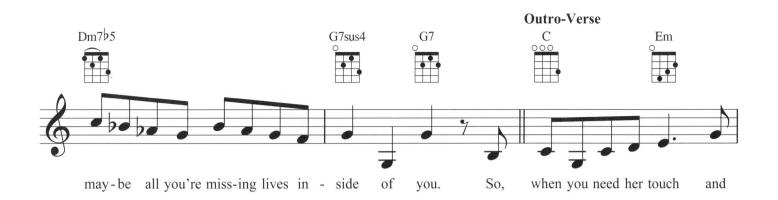

may-be all you're miss-ing lives in - side of you. So, when you need her touch and

lov - ing gaze, "gone, but not for - got - ten," is the per - fect phrase.

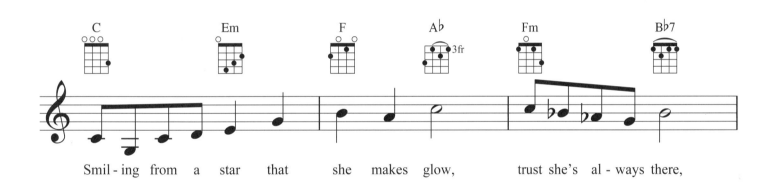

Smil - ing from a star that she makes glow, trust she's al - ways there,

watch - ing as you grow. Find her in the place where the lost things

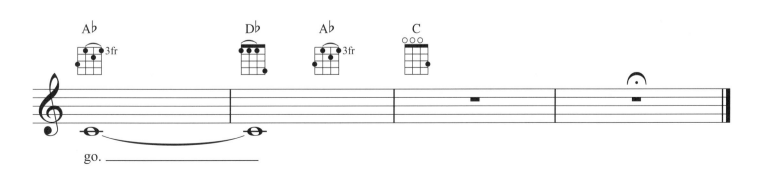

go. _____

Remember Me

(Ernesto de la Cruz)

from COCO

Music and Lyrics by Kristen Anderson-Lopez and Robert Lopez

First note

Verse
Moderately fast

ERNESTO DE LA CRUZ:

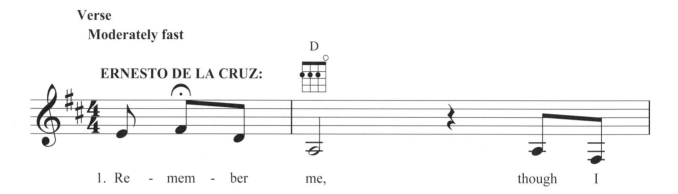

1. Re - mem - ber me, though I

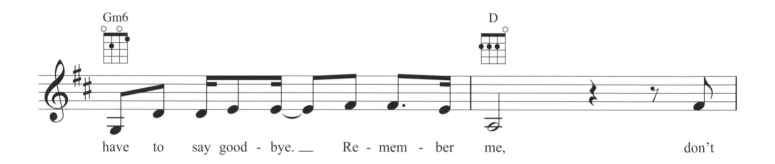

have to say good - bye. ___ Re - mem - ber me, don't

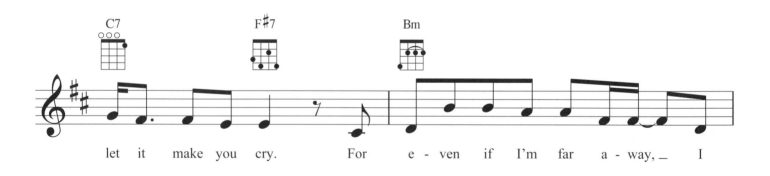

let it make you cry. For e - ven if I'm far a - way, ___ I

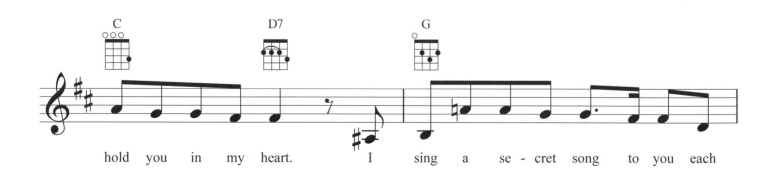

hold you in my heart. I sing a se - cret song to you each

night   we   are   a - part.   Re - mem - ber   me,   though   I

have   to   trav - el   far. ___   Re - mem - ber   me   each   time   you

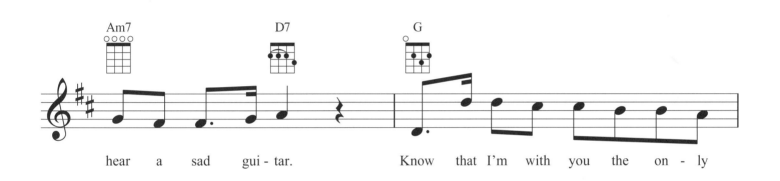

hear   a   sad   gui - tar.   Know   that   I'm   with   you   the   on - ly

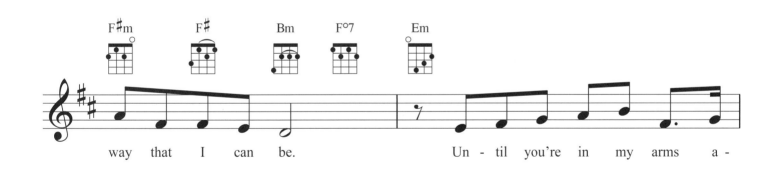

way   that   I   can   be.   Un - til   you're   in   my   arms   a -

Interlude

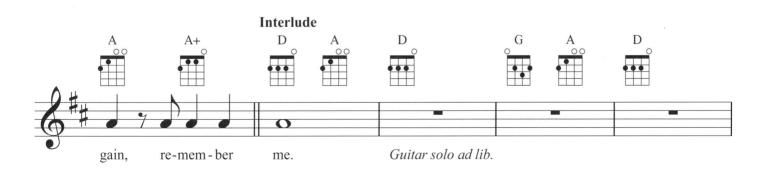

gain,   re - mem - ber   me.   *Guitar solo ad lib.*

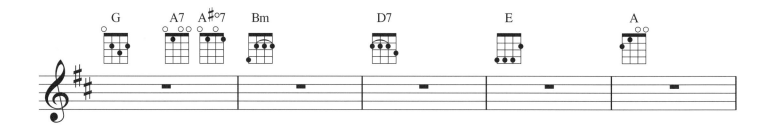

2. Re - mem - ber me, though I

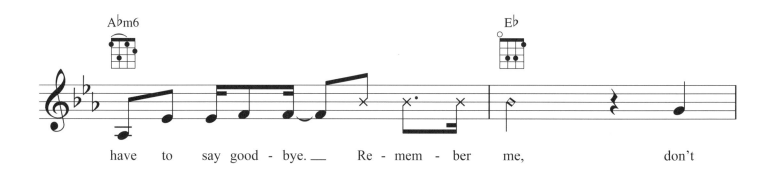

have to say good - bye. ___ Re - mem - ber me, don't

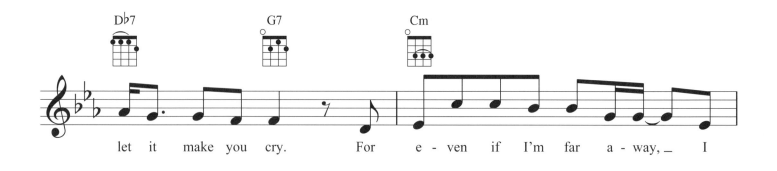

let it make you cry. For e - ven if I'm far a - way, ___ I

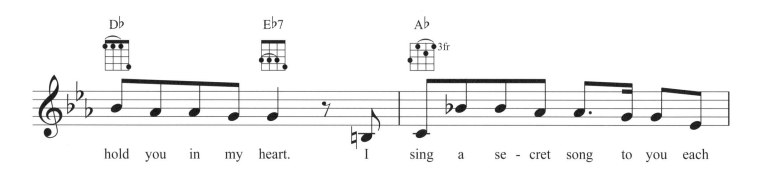

hold you in my heart. I sing a se - cret song to you each

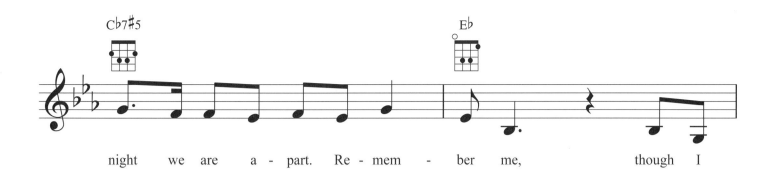

night we are a - part. Re - mem - ber me, though I

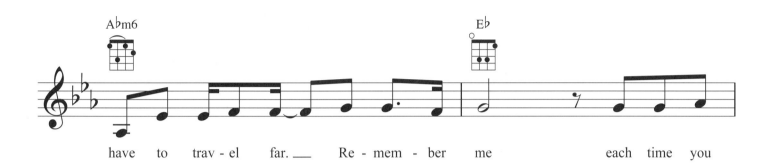

have to trav - el far.___ Re - mem - ber me each time you

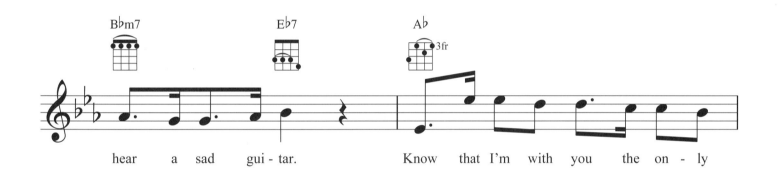

hear a sad gui - tar. Know that I'm with you the on - ly

Slowly, deliberately

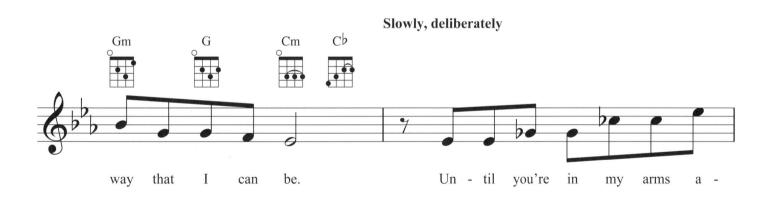

way that I can be. Un - til you're in my arms a -

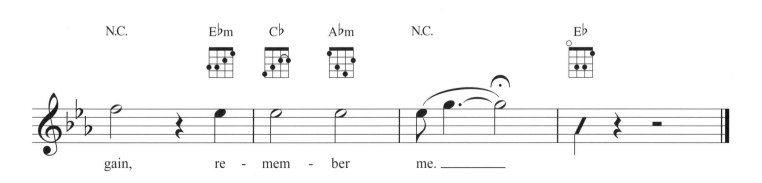

gain, re - mem - ber me.___

Some Day My Prince Will Come

from SNOW WHITE AND THE SEVEN DWARFS
Words by Larry Morey
Music by Frank Churchill

First note

Flowing

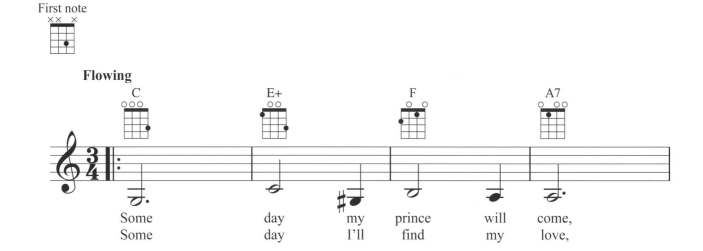

Some   day   my   prince   will   come,
Some   day   I'll   find   my   love,

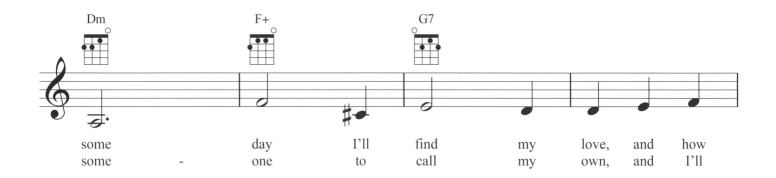

some   day   I'll   find   my   love,   and   how
some - one   to   call   my   own,   and   I'll

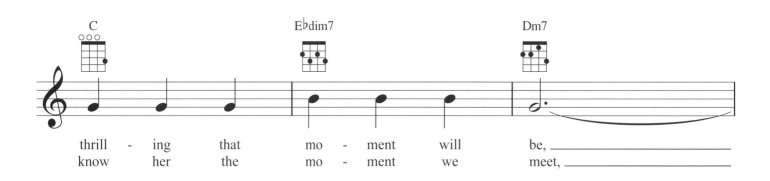

thrill - ing   that   mo - ment   will   be, _____
know   her   the   mo - ment   we   meet, _____

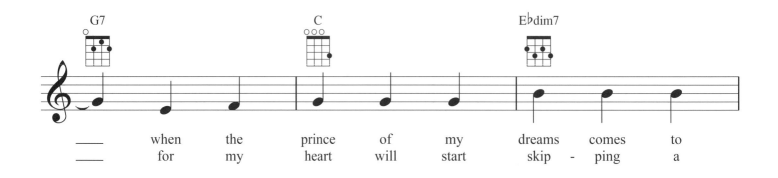

_____ when   the   prince   of   my   dreams   comes   to
_____ for   my   heart   will   start   skip - ping   a

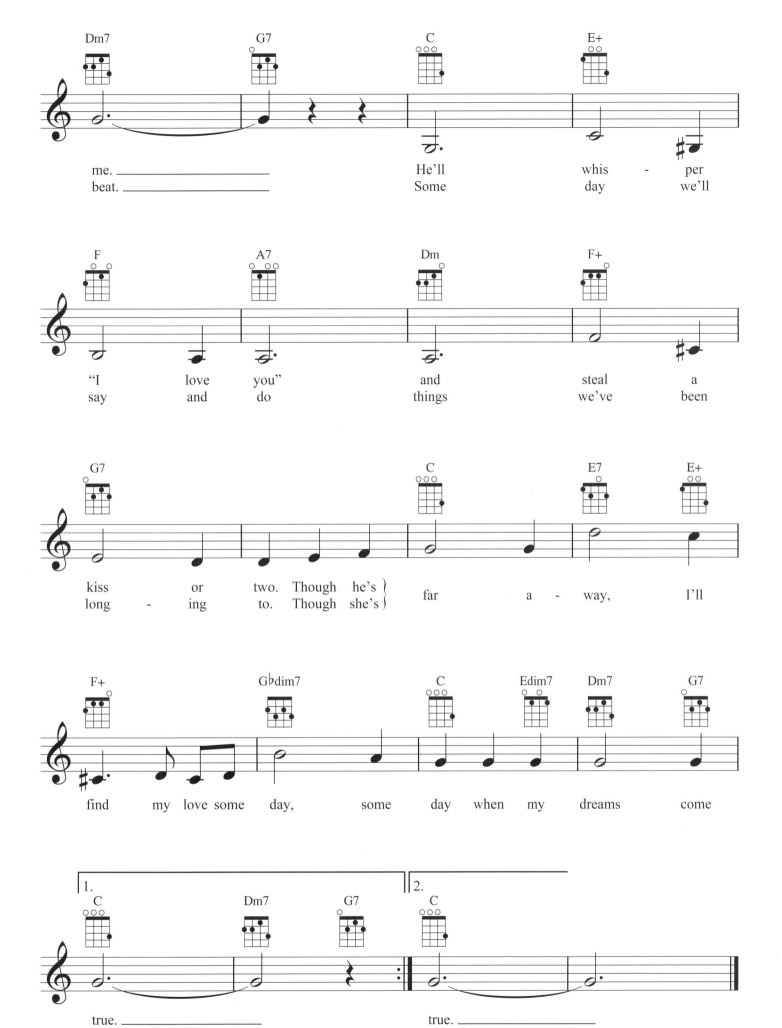

Speechless

from ALADDIN (2019)

Music by Alan Menken

Lyrics by Benj Pasek and Justin Paul

First note

Verse
Half-time feel

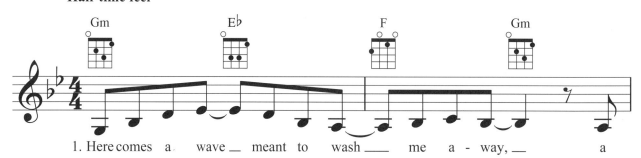

1. Here comes a wave _ meant to wash _ me a - way, _ a

tide that is tak-ing me un - der. _____ Swal - low-ing sand, _ left with noth-

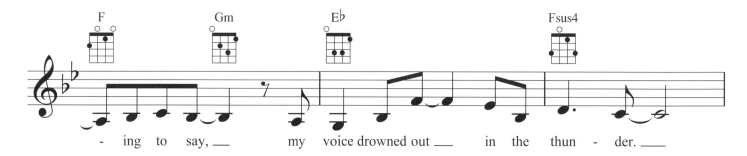

- ing to say, _ my voice drowned out _ in the thun - der. _

Pre-Chorus

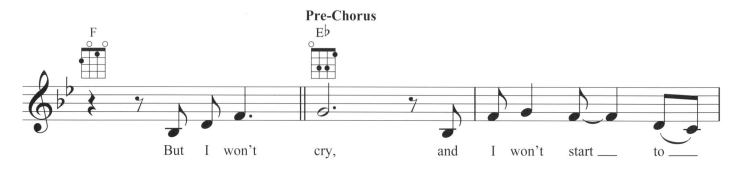

But I won't cry, and I won't start _ to _

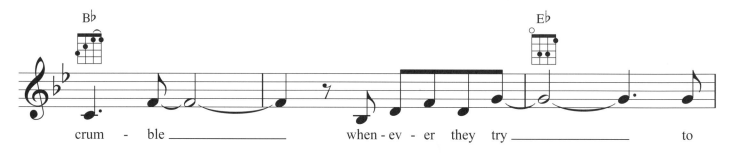

crum - ble _____ when-ev - er they try _____ to

_____ that I won't _ go _____ speech - less.

Verse

2. Writ - ten in stone, ___ ev - 'ry rule, ev - 'ry word,

cen - tu - ries old _____ and un - bend - ing.

Stay in your place, ___ bet - ter seen _____ and not heard; well,

now that sto - ry is end - ing. 'Cause

Pre-Chorus

I, I can - not start ___ to crum - ble. _____

True Love's Kiss

from ENCHANTED
Music by Alan Menken
Lyrics by Stephen Schwartz

A7 **Dm** **F** **G7**

just find who you love through true love's

Interlude

C **Em** **F** **C** **F** **Am**

kiss. *(Instrumental)*

Light Waltz, in one

D7 **G7** **C** **F#°7** **Dm7**

Ah, _____ ah, _____ ah. _____

Verse

G7 **C** **Em** **F**

___ 2. She's been dream - ing of a true love's

C **F** **G7** **Am** **D7**

kiss; and a prince she's hop - ing comes with

G7 **F** **Em** **Am**

this. That's what brings ev - er - af - ter -

ings   so   hap - py.   *(Instrumental)*

And   that's   the   rea - son   we need   lips   so

much,   for   lips   are   the   on - ly   things   that

Outro

touch.   So,   to   spend   a

life   of   end - less   bliss,   just   find   who

you   love   through   true   love's   kiss.

Supercalifragilisticexpialidocious

from MARY POPPINS

Words and Music by Richard M. Sherman and Robert B. Sherman

First note

Chorus
Brightly, in 2

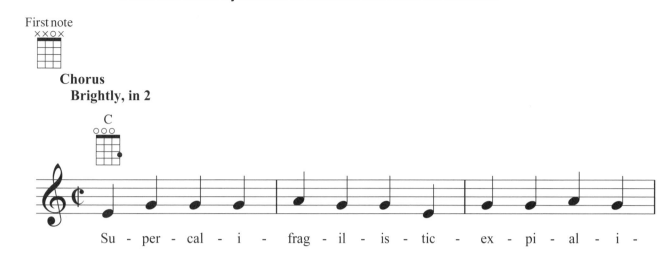

Su - per - cal - i - frag - il - is - tic - ex - pi - al - i -

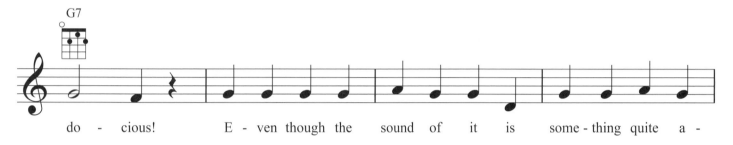

do - cious! E - ven though the sound of it is some - thing quite a -

tro - cious, if you say it loud e - nough, you'll

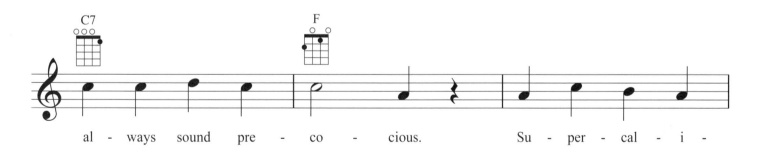

al - ways sound pre - co - cious. Su - per - cal - i -

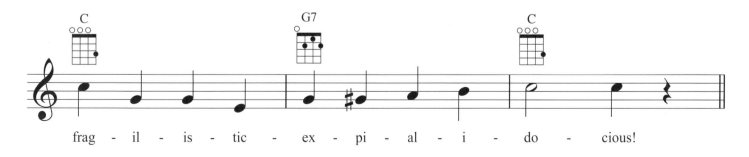

frag - il - is - tic - ex - pi - al - i - do - cious!

Interlude

Um did - dle did - dle did - dle, um did - dle ay! Um did - dle did - dle did - dle,

Verse

um did - dle ay!
1. Be - cause I was a - fraid to speak when
2. He trav - eled all a - round the world and
3. So when the cat has got your tongue, there's

I was just a lad, me fa - ther gave me
ev - 'ry - where he went he'd use his word and
no need for dis - may. Just sum - mon up this

nose a tweak and told me I was bad. But
all would say, "There goes a clev - er gent!" When
word and then you've got a lot to say. But

then one day I learned a word that saved me ach - in'
dukes and ma - 'a - ra - jas pass the time of day with
bet - ter use it care - ful - ly or it can change your

nose, the big - gest word you ev - er 'eard and
me, I say me spe - cial word and then they
life. One night I said it to me girl and

Under the Sea

from THE LITTLE MERMAID

Music by Alan Menken
Lyrics by Howard Ashman

Chorus

Such won - der - ful things sur - round you. What more __ is you
One day __ when the boss get hun - gry, guess who __ gon' be

look - in' for? Un - der the sea,
on the plate? Un - der the sea,

un - der the sea. Dar - lin', it's
un - der the sea. No - bod - y

bet - ter down __ where it's wet - ter. Take __ it from me.
beat us, fry __ us and eat us in __ fric - as - see.

Up on the shore they work __ all day. _____ Out in the
We what the land folks loves __ to cook. _____ Un - der the

sun they slave __ a - way, while we de - vot - in' full time to
sea we off __ the hook. We got no trou - bles, life is the

Bridge

_____ play the flute. The carp _____ play the harp. The plaice _____ play the bass, and they _____

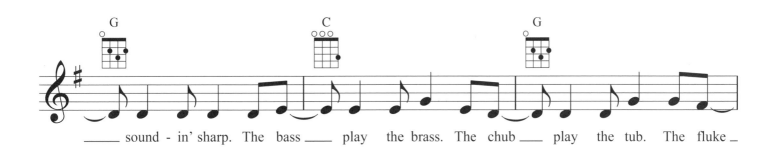

_____ sound - in' sharp. The bass _____ play the brass. The chub _____ play the tub. The fluke _____

_____ is the duke of soul. The ray, _____ he can play. The ling's _____

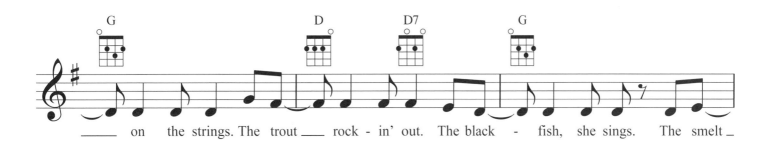

_____ on the strings. The trout _____ rock - in' out. The black - fish, she sings. The smelt _____

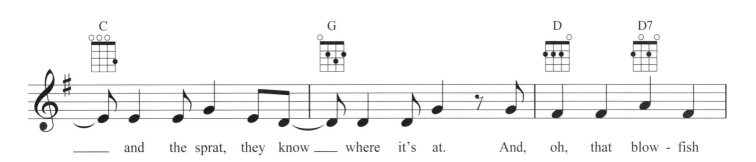

_____ and the sprat, they know _____ where it's at. And, oh, that blow - fish

Interlude

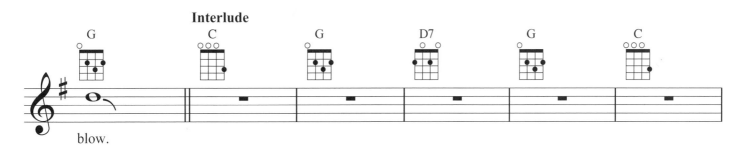

blow.

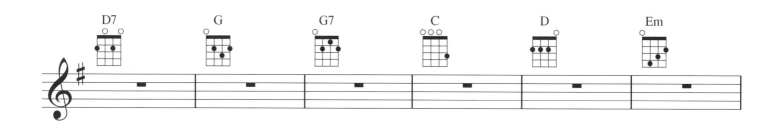

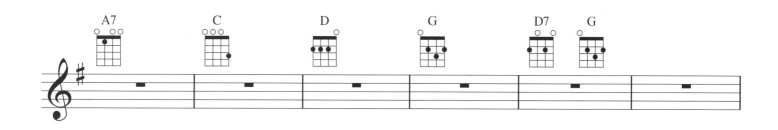

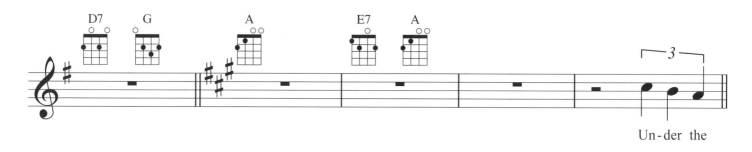

Un - der the

Chorus

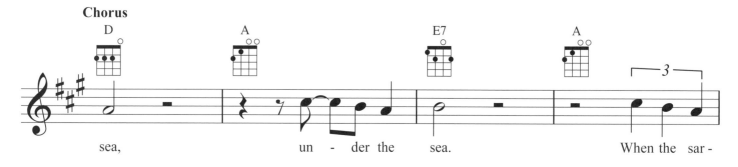

sea,   un - der the sea.   When the sar -

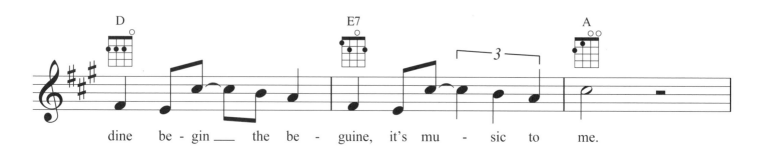

dine be - gin ___ the be - guine, it's mu - sic to me.

What do they got? A lot ___ of sand.   We got a

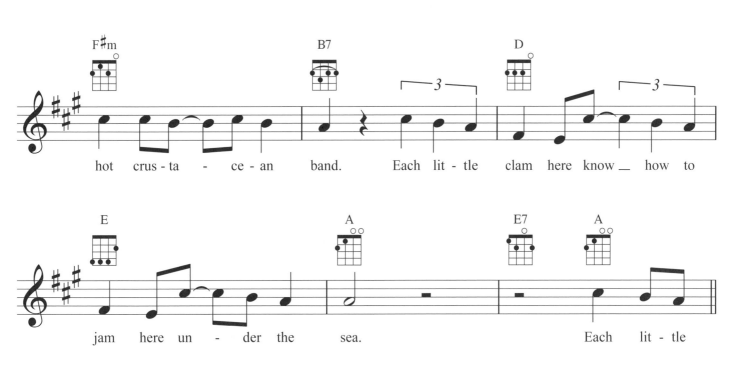

hot crus-ta-ce-an band. Each lit-tle clam here know __ how to

jam here un-der the sea. Each lit-tle

Outro

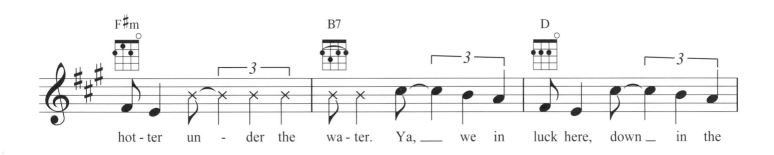

slug here cut-tin' a rug here un-der the sea.

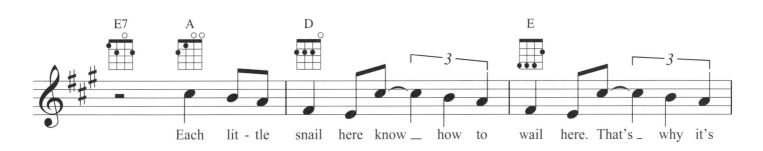

Each lit-tle snail here know __ how to wail here. That's __ why it's

hot-ter un-der the wa-ter. Ya, __ we in luck here, down __ in the

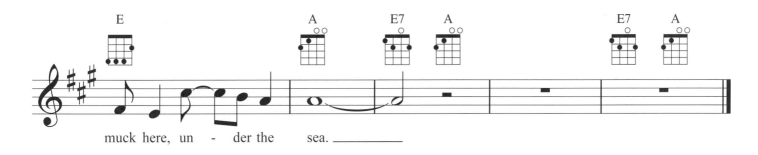

muck here, un-der the sea. _____

When You Wish Upon a Star

from PINOCCHIO
Words by Ned Washington
Music by Leigh Harline

First note

Chorus
Slowly, in 2

When you wish up - on a star,
If your wish heart up is in your your star, dream,

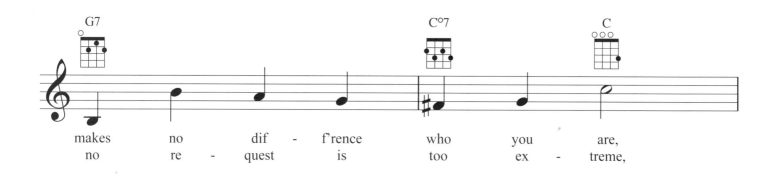

makes no dif - f'rence who you are,
no re - quest is who too ex - treme,

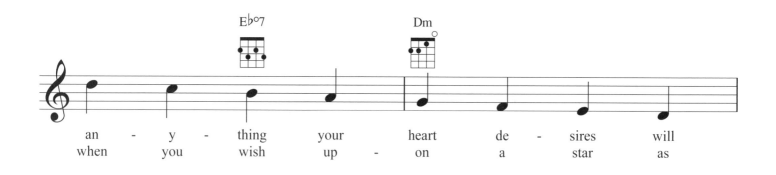

an - y - thing your heart de - sires will
when you wish up - on a star as

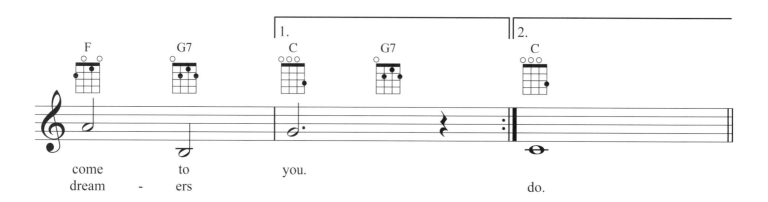

1.
come to you.
dream - ers

2.
do.

Bridge

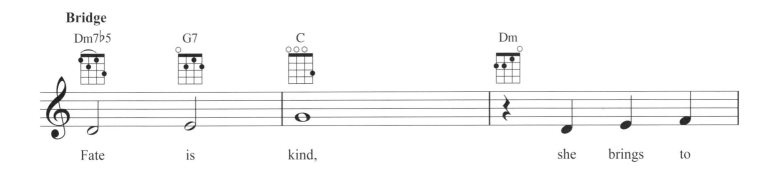

Fate is kind, she brings to

those who love the sweet ful - fill - ment of their se - cret

Outro-Chorus

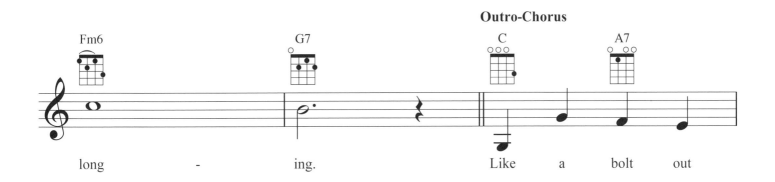

long - ing. Like a bolt out

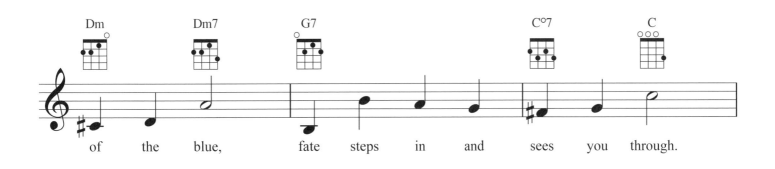

of the blue, fate steps in and sees you through.

When you wish up - on a star, your dream comes true.

Whistle While You Work

from SNOW WHITE AND THE SEVEN DWARFS
Words by Larry Morey
Music by Frank Churchill

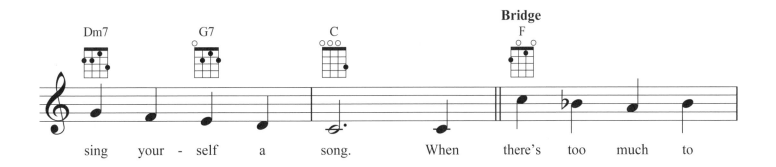

sing your - self a song. When there's too much to

do, don't let it both - er you. For -

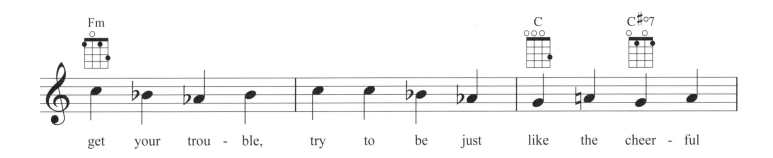

get your trou - ble, try to be just like the cheer - ful

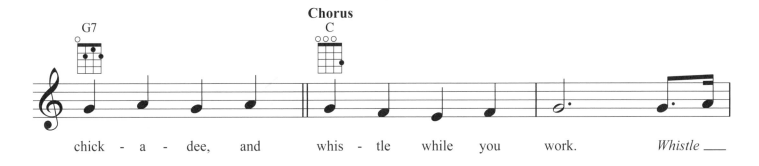

chick - a - dee, and whis - tle while you work. *Whistle* ___

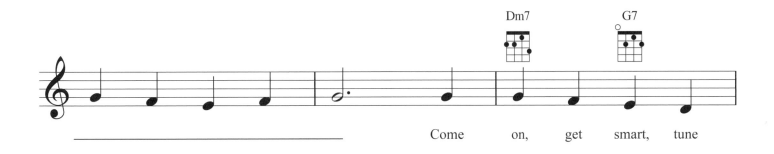

___ Come on, get smart, tune

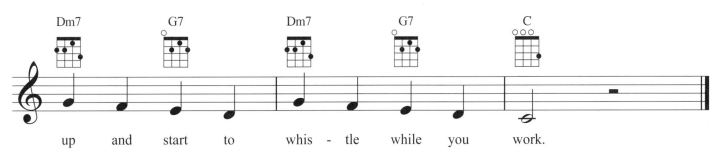

up and start to whis - tle while you work.

Who's Afraid of the Big Bad Wolf?

from THREE LITTLE PIGS
Words and Music by Frank Churchill
Additional Lyric by Ann Ronell

Who's a-fraid of the big bad wolf, big bad wolf,

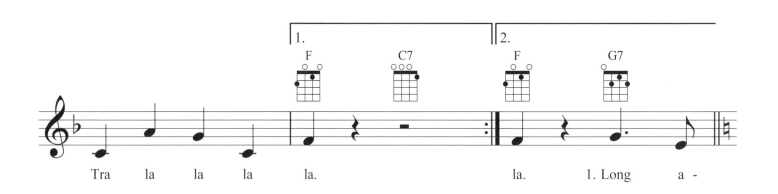

big bad wolf? Who's a-fraid of the big bad wolf?

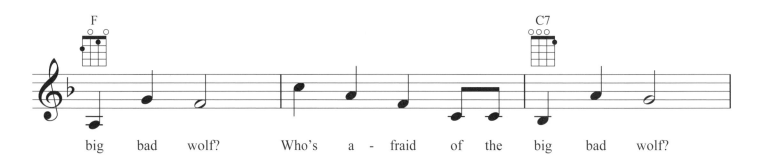

Tra la la la la. la. 1. Long a-

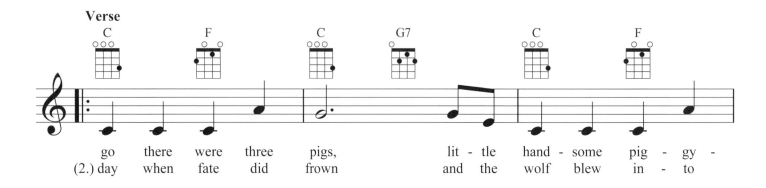

go there were three pigs, lit-tle hand-some pig-gy-
(2.) day when fate did frown and the wolf blew in-to

wigs. For the big bad, ver-y big, ver-y bad __ wolf, they __
town. With a gruff "puff, puff" __ he puffed _ just e-nough, and the

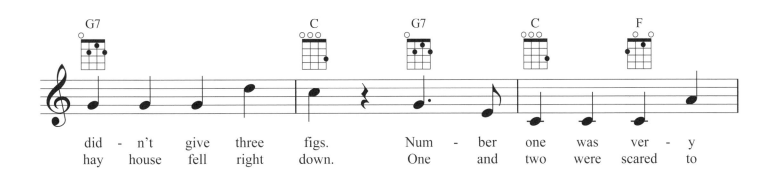

did-n't give three figs. Num-ber one was ver-y
hay house give fell right down. One and two were scared to

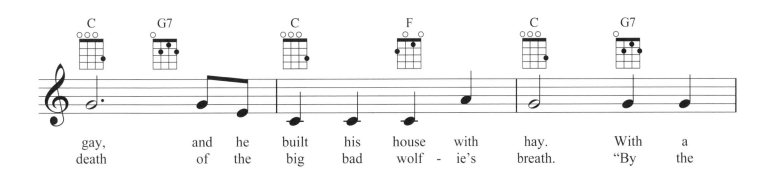

gay, and he built his house with hay. With a
death of the big his bad wolf-ie's breath. "By the

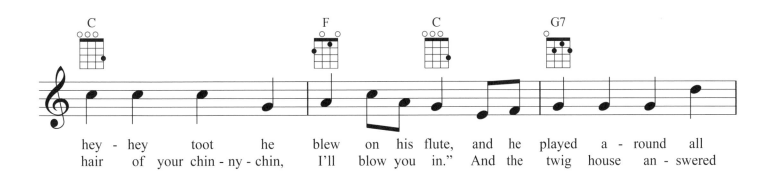

hey-hey toot he blew on his flute, and he played a-round all
hair of your chin-ny-chin, I'll blow you in." And the twig house an-swered

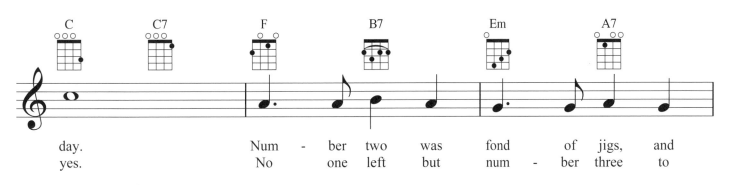

day. Num-ber two was fond of jigs, and
yes. No one left but num-ber three and to

Pre-Chorus

A Whole New World

from ALADDIN
Words by Alan Menken
Lyrics by Tim Rice

Chorus

A whole new world, _____ a new fan -
tas - tic point __ of view. ____ No one to tell us no or
where to go or say we're on - ly dream - ing. A whole new
world, _____ a daz - zling place I nev - er knew. __
____ But when I'm way up here, it's crys - tal clear that
now I'm in a whole new world with you. _____

with new ho - ri - zons to ___ pur - sue. ___ I'll chase them

an - y - where. There's time to spare. Let me share this

whole new world with you. ___ A whole new

Outro

world, ___ that's where we'll be.

A thrill - ing chase, a won - drous place for you and

me. ___

Winnie the Pooh

from THE MANY ADVENTURES OF WINNIE THE POOH

Words and Music by Richard M. Sherman and Robert B. Sherman

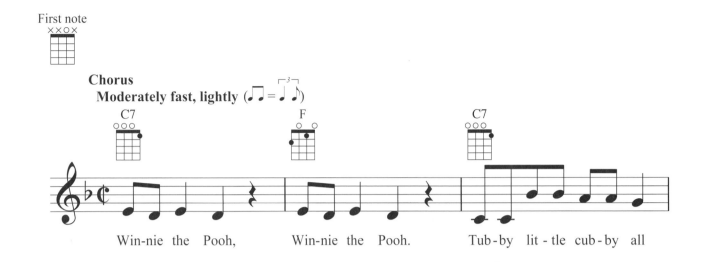

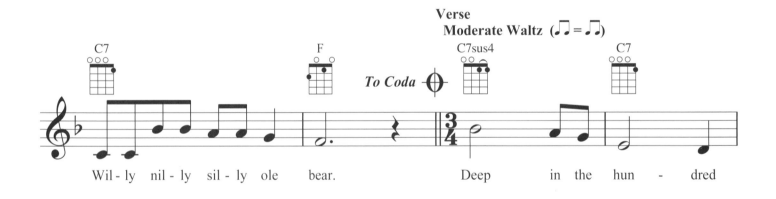

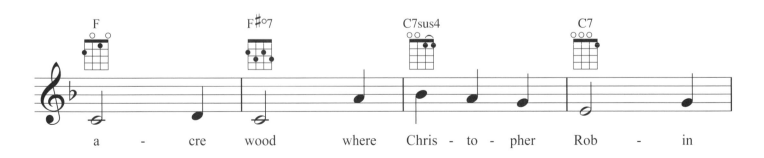

plays, _____ you will find the en - chant - ed

neigh - bor - hood of Chris - to - pher's child - hood

Pre-Chorus
Tempo I (♩♩ = ♩ ♩)

days. _____ A don-key named Ee - yore is his friend, and

Kan - ga and lit - tle Roo. There's Rab - bit and Pig - let

and there's Owl, but most of all Win - nie the Pooh.

Wil - ly nil - ly sil - ly ole bear.

Yo Ho
(A Pirate's Life for Me)

from Disney Parks' Pirates of the Caribbean attraction
Words by Xavier Atencio
Music by George Bruns

First note

Chorus
In a robust manner

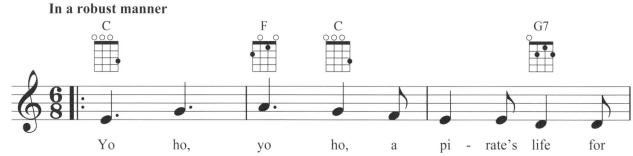

Yo ho, yo ho, a pi - rate's life for

Verse

me.
1. We pil - lage, we plun - der, we ri - fle and loot. Drink
2. We ex - tort and pil - fer, we filch ___ and sack. Drink
3. We kin - dle and char and in - flame and ig - nite. Drink

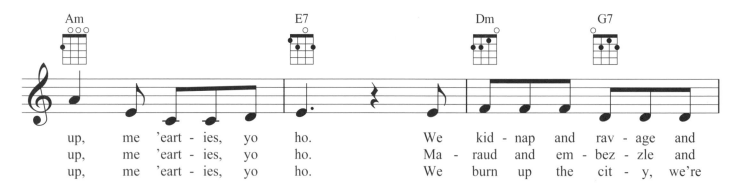

up, me 'eart - ies, yo ho. We kid - nap and rav - age and
up, me 'eart - ies, yo ho. Ma - raud and em - bez - zle and
up, me 'eart - ies, yo ho. We burn up the cit - y, we're

1., 2.

don't give a hoot. Drink up, me 'eart - ies, yo ho.
e - ven high - jack. Drink up, me 'eart - ies, yo ho.
real - ly a fright. Drink

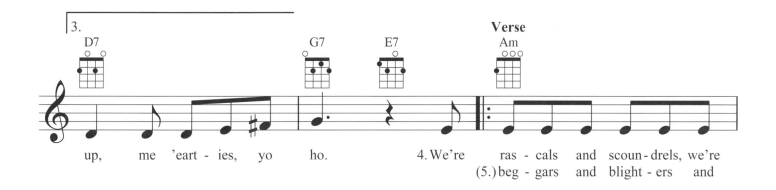

up, me 'eart-ies, yo ho.   4. We're ras-cals and scoun-drels, we're
                                        (5.) beg-gars and blight-ers and

vil-lains and knaves. Drink up, me 'eart-ies, yo ho.   We're
ne'er-do-well cads. Drink up, me 'eart-ies, yo ho.   And

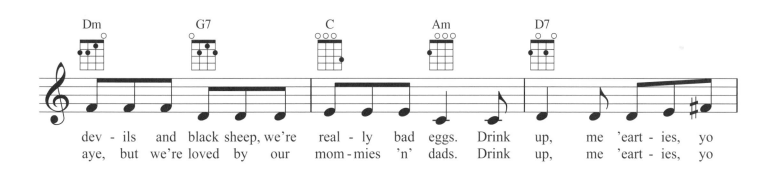

dev-ils and black sheep, we're real-ly bad eggs. Drink up, me 'eart-ies, yo
aye, but we're loved by our mom-mies 'n' dads. Drink up, me 'eart-ies, yo

Chorus

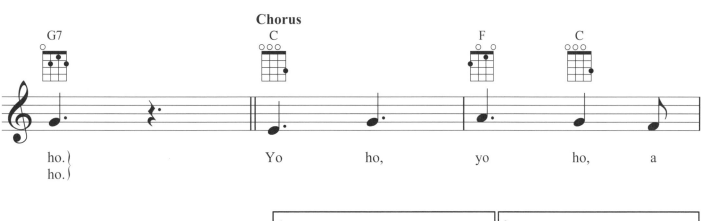

ho. ⎱
ho. ⎰   Yo ho,   yo ho,   a

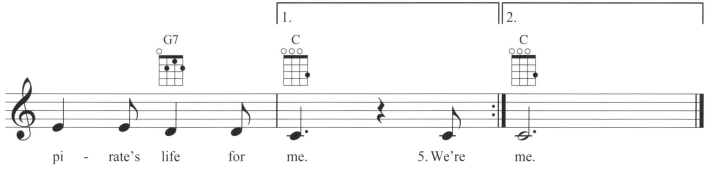

pi-rate's life for me.   5. We're   me.

You'll Be in My Heart

(Pop Version)*

from TARZAN®
Words and Music by Phil Collins

First note

1. Come, stop your cry-ing; it will be all right. __

Just take my hand, hold it tight. __ I will pro-tect you from

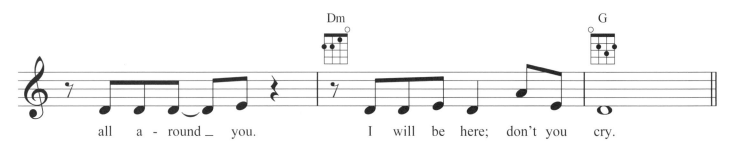

all a-round __ you. I will be here; don't you cry.

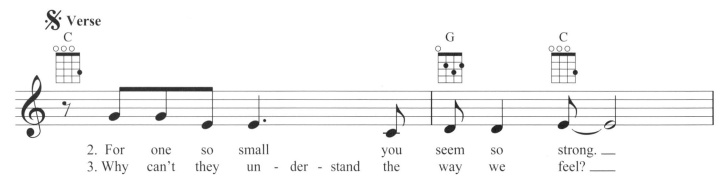

2. For one so small you seem so strong. __
3. Why can't they un-der-stand the way we feel? __

My arms will hold you, keep you safe and warm. __ This bond be-tween us
They just don't trust __ what they can't ex - plain. __ I know we're dif-f'rent, but

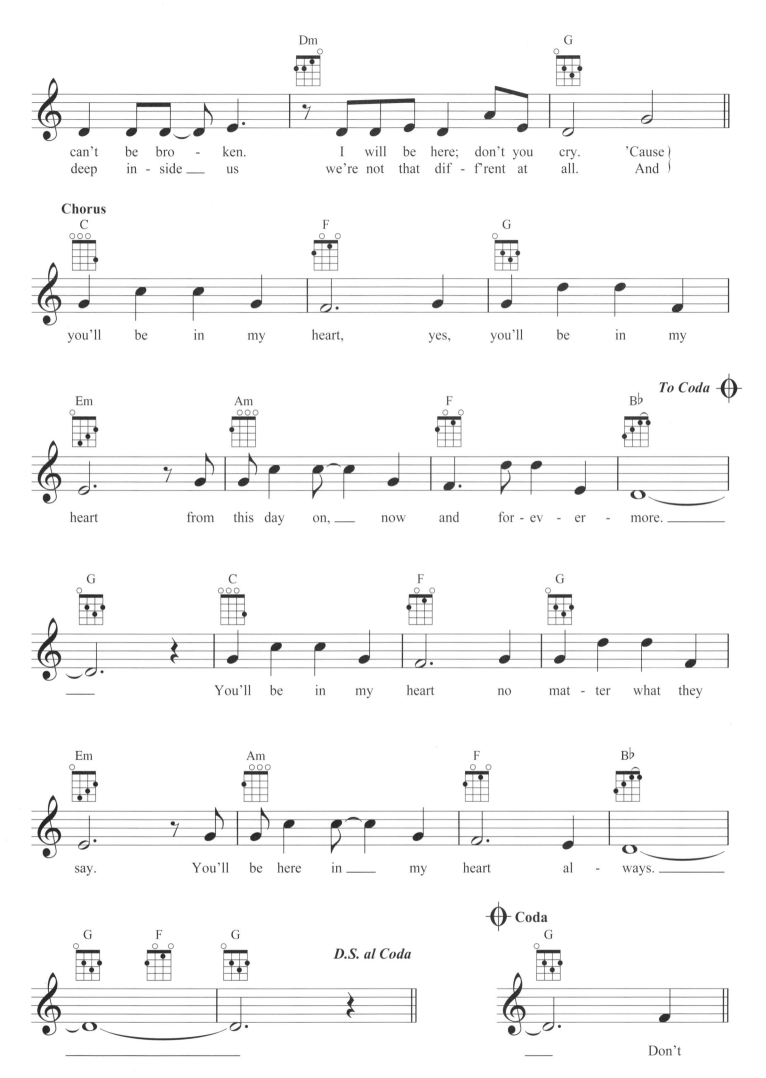

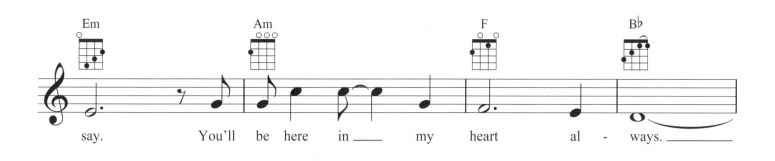

say. You'll be here in _____ my heart al - ways. _____

Outro

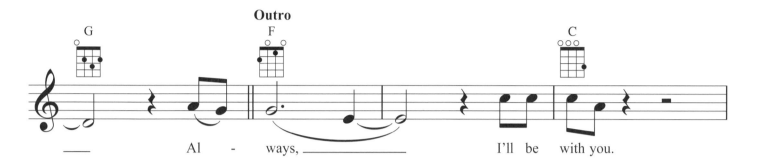

_____ Al - ways, _____ I'll be with you.

I'll be there for you al - ways, al - ways and al -

- ways. _____ Just look o - ver your shoul - der.

Just look o - ver your shoul - der. Just look

o - ver your shoul - der; I'll be there _____ al - ways. _____

You've Got a Friend in Me

from TOY STORY
Music and Lyrics by Randy Newman

Bridge

Now, some oth - er folks might be a lit - tle bit smart - er than I am,

big - ger and strong - er, too. ____ May - be. But none of them will

ev - er love __ you the way ____ I do, ____ just me and you, __ boy.

And as the years go by, ____ our friend - ship will nev - er die. ____

Outro

You're gon - na see it's our des - ti - ny. You've got a friend in me. __

You've got a friend in me. ____

Zip-A-Dee-Doo-Dah

from SONG OF THE SOUTH
Music by Allie Wrubel
Words by Ray Gilbert

First note

Chorus
Merrily

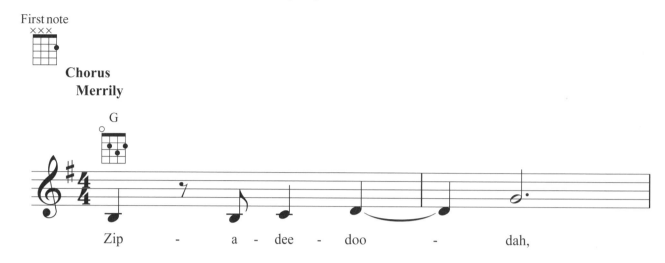

Zip - a - dee - doo - dah,

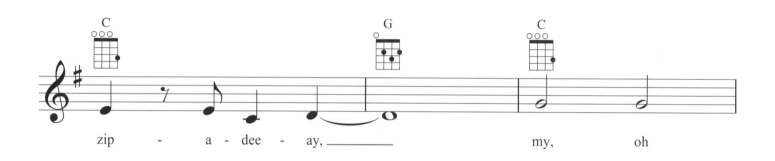

zip - a - dee - ay, _____ my, oh

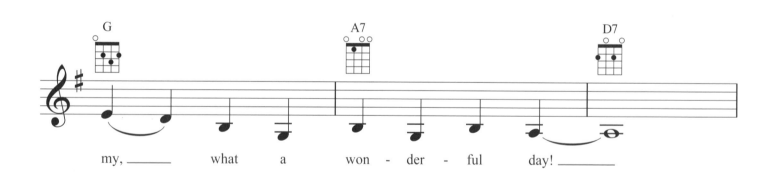

my, _____ what a won - der - ful day! _____

Plen - ty of sun - shine, head - in' my way, _____
Zip - a - dee - doo - dah, zip - a - dee - ay! _____

To Coda

zip - a - dee - doo - dah,
Won - der - ful feel - ing,

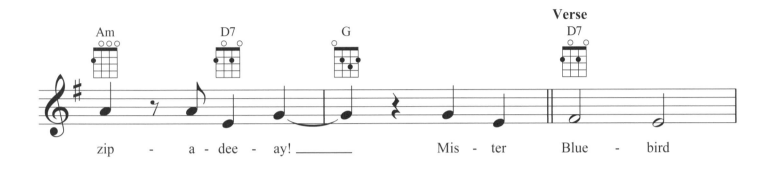

Verse

zip - a - dee - ay! _____ Mis - ter Blue - bird

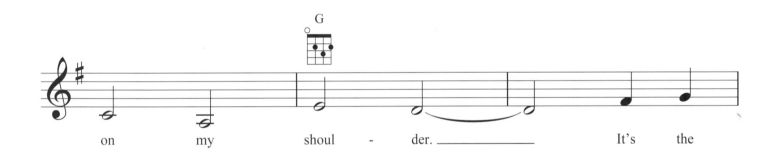

on my shoul - der. _____ It's the

truth, it's "act - ch'll," ev - 'ry - thing is

Coda

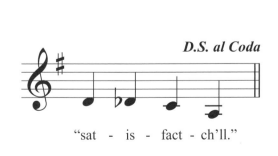

D.S. al Coda

"sat - is - fact - ch'll."

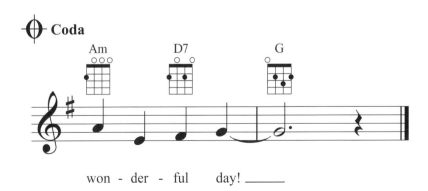

won - der - ful day! _____

When She Loved Me

from TOY STORY 2
Music and Lyrics by Randy Newman

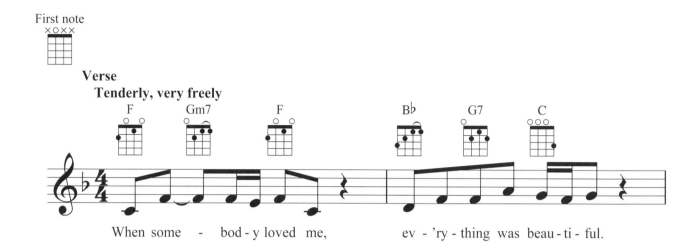

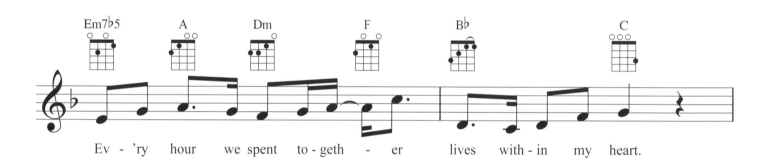

When some - bod - y loved me, ev - 'ry - thing was beau - ti - ful.

Ev - 'ry hour we spent to - geth - er lives with - in my heart.

And when she was sad, I was there to dry her tears;

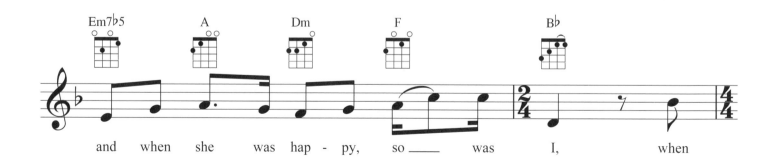

and when she was hap - py, so ___ was I, when